FULL COLOR EXPANDED EDITION

THE SECRET UFO CONTACTS OF PAUL VILLA

Interplanetary Visitors From Coma Berenices

- PLUS BONUS SECTION -

THE FRIENDSHIP CONTACT CASE

This beautiful rendering © by Carol Ann Rodriguez was inspired by the photographs of Paul Villa and other UFO contactees.

Even though they come from a long distance away, the beings Paul Villa met looked remarkably human. Art © by Carol Ann Rodriguez.

Full Color Expanded Edition

The Secret UFO Contacts of Paul Villa: Interplanetary Visitors From Coma Berenices

By Lt. Colonel Wendelle C. Stevens

Additional Material By Timothy Green Beckley, Sean Casteel and Tim R. Swartz

Copyright © 2020 by Timothy Green Beckley
dba Inner Light/Global Communications

All Rights Reserved

No part of these manuscripts may be copied or reproduced by any mechanical or digital methods and no excerpts or quotes may be used in any other book or manuscript without permission in writing by the Publisher, Inner Light/Global Communications, except by a reviewer who may quote brief passages in a review.

Published in the United States of America By
Inner Light/Global Communications
Box 753, New Brunswick, NJ 08903

Staff Members

Timothy G. Beckley, Publisher

Carol Ann Rodriguez, Assistant to the Publisher

Sean Casteel, General Associate Editor

Tim R. Swartz, Editor, Graphics, Layout

William Kern, Editorial and Art Consultant

www.conspiracyjournal.com
www.teslasecretfiles.com
Email: MrUFO8@hotmail.com

THE SECRET UFO CONTACTS OF PAUL VILLA

CONTENTS

THE COMING OF PAUL VILLA 7
THE UFOs POSE FOR PAUL VILLA 15
PREFACE 23
CHAPTER ONE 25
THE SECRET LIFE OF PAUL VILLA 26
OUR FOLLOW-UP 36
MINI-UFOS 61
CONCLUSION 90
PAUL VILLA – THE MODEST CONTACTEE 92
ITALY'S "FRIENDSHIP" CASE 96
ABOUT THE AUTHOR 102

THE SECRET UFO CONTACTS OF PAUL VILLA

Timothy Green Beckley UFO & Paranormal Pioneer

Publisher Tim Beckley catches a hot breeze as he searches for spot where one of Paul Villa's UFOs is said to have landed. (Photo by Helen Hovey)

Tim Beckley has had so many careers that even his own girlfriend doesn't know what he does for a living.

Timothy Green Beckley has been described as the Hunter Thompson of UFOlogy by the editor of "*UFO magazine*," Nancy Birnes.

Since an early age his life has more or less revolved around the paranormal. At the age of three his life was saved by an invisible force. The house he was raised in was thought to be haunted. His grandfather saw a headless horseman. Beckley underwent out of body experiences starting at age six, and saw his first of three UFOs when he was ten. Since then he has had two more sightings including an attempt to communicate with one of these objects in the UK.

Beckley is the author of many books including "***Deja Vu UFOs Over And Over Again***," "***Alien Strongholds on Earth: Secret UFO Bases Exist All Around Us***," "***The Matrix Control System of Philip K. Dick And The Paranormal Synchronicities of Timothy Green Beckley***," and "***David Bowie, UFOs, Witchcraft, Cocaine and Paranoia - Full Color Version: The Occult Saga of Walli Elmlark - The "Rock and Roll" Witch of New York***."

THE COMING OF PAUL VILLA
By Timothy Green Beckley

I'll never forget the box full of postcards that arrived in the mail from UFO publisher, convention sponsor and flying saucer promoter Gabriel Green who lived down in Yucca Valley, California, and was the chief supporter of the New Age branch of the flying saucer movement. His *"International UFO Journal"* was the journalistic voice of the contactees who spoke of friendly aliens, and he wrote books about their Space Brother friends.

The postcards were the slick glossy kind that you would pay a quarter for if you wanted to send a greeting to your friends back home while traveling out of town.

Gabriel Green founder of the Amalgamated Flying Saucer Clubs of America personally paid for the print of a hundred thousand glossy postcards depicting a close up shot of one of Paul Villa's famous UFOs.

THE SECRET UFO CONTACTS OF PAUL VILLA

But the friends who were onboard this fine disc shaped craft, complete with porthole-like windows, had to be cruising a long way from Route 66.

The picture on the post card taken by one Paul Villa of New Mexico was almost too realistic looking to be legitimate. Many of the serious-type UFOlogists took it as a hoax, but they did not have the opportunity to see the full array of pictures taken by this gentlemen whom everyone said was almost a recluse, hiding out in his trail before the men in black – or some other sinister group – attempted to burn his living quarters to the ground.

Probably a hundred thousand of the Paul Villa postcards were distributed. For a long while this was the most frequently published picture of a UFO gracing many a newspaper and periodical even if it had nothing to do with the context of the story. Gabe was going to see that the post card got distributed far and wide because he had a great interest in what Paul Villa had to say about his contacts with extraterrestrials from Coma Berenices.

When UFO abductee, and channeler Diane Tessman visited Gabe in his trailer, we couldn't help but notice that the photos of Paul Villa were hung up on the walls, he revered them so.

There are some who thought Mr. Green was overly passionate in putting his faith into what Villa and the other contactees had to say. So "strange" were the descriptions of their ongoing encounters and contacts which included claiming to meet highly advanced beings from the other side of the cosmos and in some cases actually going for rides in their craft from the stars.

WHO WAS GABRIEL GREEN?

Born at Whittier in 1924, Gabriel Green was a life-long Southern Californian, the first two-thirds of his life spent in greater Los Angeles, the remaining in the Inland Empire. After graduating Whittier Union High School in 1942, Green began studying at the Los Angeles Art Center School of Photography. But his career aspirations were put on hold following his being drafted into the Navy. At war's end, Green returned to civilian life and resumed his study, coming to operate a photography studio and obtaining a job in the Los Angeles school system.

THE SECRET UFO CONTACTS OF PAUL VILLA

Gabe Green at Giant Rock some time in the 1960s. (Photo credit: Joe Fex-APEX Research)

As the flying saucer movement became popularized, Green leapt in feet first, organizing the Los Angeles Interplanetary Study Group in 1956. The group's earliest activities, spearheaded by Green himself, included the publicizing of Richard Miller's Mon-Ka recordings, "made by mental telepathy from Mars," on Los Angeles television and radio stations. The tapes featured "a celestial-sounding voice" promising that at 10:30 PM (PST) on November 7, 1956, a Martian saucer would fly over the city; and, further, "the men from Mars [will] speak to us on the wavelength of a station if that station will cease its programming." Despite Green's attempts, most stations did not cease broadcasting that night, and no message was to be heard by the millions of Angelenos.

Through the last years of the 1950s, Green would continue his media push, becoming a regular attendee and speaker at popular saucer events, including the Giant Rock conventions, and making guest appearances on a variety of interview shows and talk radio programs. He likewise undertook an expansion of his organizational efforts, launching the Amalgamated Flying Saucer Clubs of America (AFSCA), as a successor to his study group in 1959, and put together a national newsletter and UFO conventions under the new banner, opening yet new venues to the Space People and their Earth contacts. Green's efforts were not, however, limited to media appearances and newsletters: like George Van Tassel, he was directly involved as a trance medium and contactee, channeling messages from the Space People himself. He led UFO circles in past life regressions and taught individuals how they too could make psychic contacts with far-distant beings.

THE SECRET UFO CONTACTS OF PAUL VILLA

Paul Villa's spaceship photo was used to promote this spectacular Flying Saucer Convention which cost only $2.00 a day to attend.

Political button for Gabriel Green's 1960 Presidential campaign, featuring the slogan "ABE IN 1860, GABE IN 1960" (comparing himself to Abraham "Abe" Lincoln)

When the 1960 election cycle came around, Green made his first foray into politics, launching a campaign for the Presidency, competing against fellow Whittier-born Richard Nixon and the Democratic rival, John F. Kennedy. Though not formally listed on any ballot, Green nonetheless put together a full platform, covering a range of economic and social policies based on information received from the Space People, and made modest campaigning efforts, though largely limited to his California turf, where he ran a full-page spread in the Los Angeles Mirror News. Despite early enthusiasm, the campaign did not last, and Green withdrew in October, giving his endorsement to Kennedy.

In November of the same year, Green travelled with Helen Isabel Sibert, his companion and supporter, to Las Vegas, Nevada, where the two were wed. The couple remained together until her passing in early May of 1970; Green never remarried.

Not dissuaded by the cool reception to his previous presidential aspirations, Green launched a fresh political campaign in 1962, this time to become the Democratic Party's California nominee for the United States Senate. Positioning himself as an anti-nuclear testing candidate – a message frequently repeated by many saucerians in their claimed messages from the Space People - Green ultimately placed second in the convention balloting with just over 8% of the vote, far behind popular California State Senator

THE SECRET UFO CONTACTS OF PAUL VILLA

Richard Richards (who, in turn, lost to Republican incumbent Thomas H. Kuchel).

Putting politics behind him, Green returned his focus to the work of promoting the messages of the Space People, from all their Earthly voices. The sixties saw several new stories come through Green's network to the pages of the AFSCA newsletters: Bob Renaud's reports of contact with Korendor; Paul Villa's photos of saucers from Coma Berenices (which became a public image of AFSCA, widely distributed as promotional postcards); and Green's own claims to connections with John F. Kennedy and Robert F. Kennedy via the Alpha Centauri contact, Renton. In addition to this newslettering, Green's first book (co-written by Warren Smith) was published in 1967 by Popular Library— a slim paperback collection entitled "**Let's Face Facts about Flying Saucers**," featuring a quick-fire selection of short reports on UFOs, their witnesses and contactees, and related Fortean events.

Despite boasting of early success and a wide membership during the early sixties, public enthusiasm for flying saucers had begun to dissipate by the end of the decade. Green's efforts were scaled back substantially, and he ended his run on the regular newsletter in favor of sporadic information bulletins.

World famous UFO abductee and channeler Diane Tessman stands with Gabe in his Yucca Valley residence while Paul Villa photos adorn the wall behind them.

THE SECRET UFO CONTACTS OF PAUL VILLA

In 1972, Green took part in his second and final presidential campaign, this time as the nominee of Kirby Hensley's Universal Party, with fellow saucerian Daniel Fry as his vice-presidential running mate. This time around Green was registered on the ballot – in Iowa – but his efforts garnered less success and less press than either of his previous campaigns. It was to be Green's last hurrah in the political arena, ending with a paltry 199 votes tallied.

After a lifetime in Los Angeles, Green retired in the mid-seventies to Yucca Valley, near Giant Rock and the original nexus of the Saucerian movement. He continued his work as a medium, relating messages from the Space People and Ashtar Command (including Master Hilarion) to their true believers, and as an organizer, remaining an active member of the UFO community until his passing in September 2001. Life story courtesy https://hatch.kookscience.com/wiki

Before his passing we purchased the rights of a book Col. Wendelle Stevens had compiled on Paul Villa. What you are reading is the first full color edition of what was originally published as **"UFO Contact from Coma Berenesis."** We have tried to provide the sharpest images of Paul Villa's photos and any added material to assist in your being able to make an educated judgment as to the validity of the photos and of the story Paul told to those willing to listen.

PAUL DONGO COMMENTS

March 8, 2018

Paul Villa photos. The first IS a huge ship. He has others that I have somewhere that are not in circulation for many years that I got from a researcher Villa said that they landed one day and told him they were from Coma Berenices. They were human and could speak any Earth language.

As I said before my specialty is Extraterrestrial humans. I have come so very close to direct contact with them. They certainly know who I am - I have been after them long enough. Stories...I have plenty. They are awesome beyond anything I could say!! They pick the time and place no matter what we do. The big ship is just over three hundred feet in diameter.

THE SECRET UFO CONTACTS OF PAUL VILLA

This UFO photograph by Paul Villa has been used in countless books and magazines...yet few know the fascinating story behind it.

Area UFO 51 June 3, 2017
INVALUABLE GRAPHIC TESTIMONY

June 16th, 1963, Albuquerque, New Mexico, one of the world's most impressive "UFO" photo sequences, 54 years ago in New Mexico, farmer Paul Villa was able to capture a Kodak camera a short distance away. Great sharpness, the photographs achieved by Villa exposed the metallic structure of the Flying Disc, as well as its incredible evolutions in the air, the base and the dome of the object are perfectly distinguishable, as well as the area "Little windows" right in the middle of the Object, Paul managed to immortalize the historic encounter that happened more than half a century ago.

Today these "Machines" continue to surprise us...they are capable of traveling from one universe to another, performing the most unusual maneuvers, overcoming any airspace, suddenly changing trajectory, hovering for hours at will. These artifacts that are part of the so-called UFO phenomena have left a record of their presence for almost seven uninterrupted decades, it is time to accept this irrefutable extraterrestrial reality.

COMPLETE PHOTOGRAPHIC SEQUENCE: THE VARIATION OF COLOR IS SO THAT SOME IMAGES WERE TAKEN FROM OUR PERSONAL FILE, TO BE ABLE TO SHARE THE COMPLETE SEQUENCE.

THE SECRET UFO CONTACTS OF PAUL VILLA

16 June 1963, 15:30, Peralta, New Mexico. Photo number 7, the last in this sequence taken by Paul Villa, shows the ship on edge as it began ascent for its departure. APRO said this proves this is just a plastic model stuck on the end of the limb. We do not agree with them.

THE UFOs POSE FOR PAUL VILLA
By Sean Casteel

Like the legendary Swiss contactee, Billy Meier, Paul Villa was an unassuming gentleman of modest means who happened to capture some striking UFO photos. Villa had no axe to grind and no desire for publicity or fame. As so often happens in the world of UFO encounters, Villa did not find the flying saucer phenomenon; it found him.

Villa told UFO investigators that he would receive a telepathic message telling him to be at a certain location, usually somewhere near his home in Albuquerque, New Mexico. When he arrived at the designated place, the alien ships would essentially "pose" for him while he took photos with a Japanese-made camera and standard Kodak film.

The result of those efforts is a beautiful series of full color photos depicting the flying saucers in all their glory. Inner Light/Global Communications has previously published a book called "***The Secret Life of Paul Villa***" that includes 20 pages of the very convincing photos as well as a fascinating background text written by veteran UFO researcher Wendelle Stevens, who followed the Villa case closely for several years. Stevens makes a very strong argument for the authenticity of the photos, noting the following features:

1. They are quite sharp, compared to most saucer photos seen up to that time, which was the 1960s through the 1970s.
2. The image size of the saucers is large enough to show good detail without the extreme graininess that comes when enlarging other UFO photos of less quality.
3. There is a series of photos, instead of just one photo, which provides more details for examination.

THE SECRET UFO CONTACTS OF PAUL VILLA

4. Villa's truck is in the foreground of some of the photos, providing a known object with which to compare the size of the saucer and to judge its distance away.
5. The degree of sharpness of other objects in the near foreground and clouds and trees in the distance indicates that the object had to be very large in order to achieve the depth of field observed to exist in the photos, thereby ruling out the possibility that a small model may have been used to fake the photos.

UFO photo analysis expert Jim Dilettoso and Col. Wendelle Stevens discuss the Paul Villa case. It was Col. Stevens who originally published the Paul Villa story in a hardcover edition.

THE SECRET UFO CONTACTS OF PAUL VILLA

Apolinar (Paul) Villa

THE MAN HIMSELF

Paul Villa was born on September 24, 1916, in Albuquerque, of Native-American/Spanish descent. While he did not complete the tenth grade, he had a good working knowledge of mathematics, physics, electricity and mechanics and was particularly gifted at detecting defects in engines and generators. His wife, Eunis, was a "war bride" from Germany; the couple met when Villa was serving as a sergeant in the U.S. Army occupational forces after the war. He brought Eunis back from Europe, and they settled in Southern California.

THE SECRET UFO CONTACTS OF PAUL VILLA

COMING TO KNOW THE SPACEMEN

Villa said he first spoke with spacemen in 1953 when he worked for the Department of Water and Power in Los Angeles. While on the job one day in Long Beach, he had a strong urge to go down to the beach, a feeling he did not then understand. There he met a man about seven feet tall. Villa's first impulse was to run away, but the man called him by name and told him many personal things about himself.

"He knew everything I had in my mind," Villa said, "and he told me many things that had taken place in my life. He then told me to look out beyond the reef. I saw a metallic-looking, disc-shaped object that seemed to be floating on the water. Then the spaceman asked me if I would like to go aboard the craft and look around. I went with him."

For Villa, the aliens were entirely human-looking, though more uniformly attractive than Earth people and definitely more refined in face and form. They took Villa on a tour of the saucer and confided in him that the whole galaxy to which Earth belongs is a grain of sand on a huge beach compared to the unfathomable number of inhabited bodies in the entire universe. They said their craft are constantly active over our planet and that they are here on a friendly mission to help Earth people.

THE PHOTOS BEGIN

The extraterrestrials spoke to Villa in his native Spanish but also spoke English fluently with him as well. They told him they had been observing the development of our "dubious civilization" from observation platforms on our Moon, Mars and Venus. As his contact experiences continued through the years, Villa was eventually invited to photograph the ships, and the aliens began to actually "pose" for that purpose. They flew their craft slowly and hovered as Villa snapped away.

Villa's photos first came to light when some of them were published by Gabriel Green, a controversial contactee in his own right, in Green's "UFO International Journal" in October 1965. At the time, the photos were greeted with some suspicion, even within the UFO community. Coral Lorenzen, who cofounded, along with her husband, Jim, the now defunct Aerial Phenomena

THE SECRET UFO CONTACTS OF PAUL VILLA

Research Organization (APRO), visited Villa at his home and asked him pointblank how he had faked the photos.

Villa responded, sarcastically, "Well, my dear lady, you just make yourself a model and toss it in the air and photograph it."

Wendelle Stevens later wrote that such a deception is not easily carried out. In fact, he tried doing it himself and, by the third photo, his model was ruined. It was also impossible to get the model in the correct attitude and angle simply by tossing it up in front of the camera.

The photos Villa took are breathtaking to look at and do appear to show actual flying saucers set against lovely desert scenery. There are different types of ships from photo to photo, which is consistent with UFO witness accounts since the 1940s and has led some analysts to think we are being visited by several different alien races and civilizations. That theory accounts for the many types of occupants reported, from the grays to the reptilians to the blonde, human-looking Nordics.

AN UNHAPPY CASE OF FAME

The notoriety that came with being "chosen" to take the photos did not make life easy for Villa, however. He suffered many instances of harassment, including an incident that happened when he stopped off at a local tavern on his way home from work. As Villa was sipping his beer, a complete stranger walked up to him and said, "So you're the nut that said he is talking to spacemen?" The stranger next punched Villa in the nose, drawing blood.

Villa never forgot that moment of genuine violence. He was often forced to move his wife and household to new locations after such incidents, which included neighbors attacking his mobile home and even some very frightening visits from the dreaded Men-In-Black. People who found him in Albuquerque, where he had relocated his family from Los Angeles after the photos appeared in the "UFO International Journal," took things from around his home for souvenirs. The thoughtless interlopers infuriated him and the incidents necessitated another move, this time to an obscure small town in the remote desert south of Albuquerque.

THE SECRET UFO CONTACTS OF PAUL VILLA

Villa died of stomach cancer in 1980 at age 64 and was buried in Santa Fe. Some of his photos were never made public, including a series that was reportedly taken on another planet. Wendelle Stevens writes that he had lost touch with Eunis Villa and appealed to readers for any information they had that would enable him to contact her and get a look at those rumored, long lost photos. We may never know everything the UFO occupants revealed to Paul Villa, but the idea that there is further photographic evidence to be seen is certainly a tantalizing one.

ABOUT THE AUTHOR: Sean Casteel is a freelance journalist who has been writing about UFOs, alien abduction and many other paranormal subjects since 1989. Sean's writing appeared in many UFO- and paranormal-related magazines, including "*UFO Magazine*," "*Tim Beckley's UFO Universe*," "*Fate*," "*Mysteries Magazine*," and "*Open Minds Magazine*," most of which are now defunct but were a major part of a thriving UFO press in their heyday. Magazines in the UK, Italy, Romania and Australia have also published Sean's work.

Sean has written or contributed to over 30 books for Global Communications and Inner Light Publications, all of which are available from Amazon.com. Sean's books include "**The Heretic's UFO Guidebook**," which analyzes a selection of Gnostic Christian writings and their relationship to the UFO phenomenon, and "**Signs and Symbols of the Second Coming**," in which he interviews several religious and paranormal experts about how prophecies of the Second Coming of Christ may be fulfilled.

To view and purchase books Sean has written or contributed to, visit his Amazon author page at: www.amazon.com/author/seancasteel

THE SECRET UFO CONTACTS OF PAUL VILLA

UFO Contact From
COMA BERENESIS
The Paul Villa Story

Peralta, New Mexico, 16 June 1963, 300' diameter craft from Coma Berenices.

By
Apolinar Villa – Wendelle Stevens

Original cover of "The Paul Villa Story" by Wendelle Stevens.

THE SECRET UFO CONTACTS OF PAUL VILLA

UFO Contact From COMA BERENESIS
The Paul Villa Story
By

Apolinar Villa – Wendelle Stevens

Bernalillo, NM, 18 April 1965, Apolinar Villa. UFO Beam set fire.

- Long term contacts since youth, followed change of location –
- Many face-to face contacts, as well as telepathic --
- Several trips aboard the alien ship, even to another planet –
- Took many series of UFO photographs of posed ships –
- Frequently attacked by uninformed and ignorant debunkers –
- Passed discrete information to NASA Controller –

THE SECRET UFO CONTACTS OF PAUL VILLA

PREFACE

Very little has ever been written about Apolinar Villa and his remarkable long-term ongoing UFO contacts with alien extraterrestrial human beings and his several remarkable series of photographs of the posed alien ships.

His contacts began, like most others, with sightings, then an awareness of their presence when they were here. This eventually developed into face-to face contact and personal interaction with them, the extraterrestrials.

When they invited him to bring his camera, a simple Japanese 120 box version, they flew their ships slowly, hovered, and posed the craft for good pictures, which he did get in series and sequence. Handicapped by a slow shutter speed and a simple low resolution lens, he nevertheless managed to get a number of excellent color photographs.

Coming shortly after George Adamski he was attacked by the usual debunkers, simply because he got some unwanted attention. He, like many others before and since, decided he did not need uninformed, self-styled experts to tell him what was true or not, because he already had his own truths, implicitly valid in his own mind and memory and in the photographs he had taken, and simply did not care what the debunkers underactive minds told them about his case.

Paul Villa sought no attention and tried his best to keep a low profile, and his business to himself. He was not too successful at this as he had to move twice to escape his unwelcome followers.

The only publication in any depth at all on this case was done by Gabriel Green in his *UFO International* journal, Number 23 for October 1965.

This then is a summary of what we do know about this truly enigmatic man, and his contribution to the lore of the UFO phenomenon.

If anybody can put me in touch with Eunis Villa, I shall be forever grateful and more of this fantastic story may then be told.

Wendelle Stevens

THE SECRET UFO CONTACTS OF PAUL VILLA

Coma Berenices is an ancient asterism in the northern sky and is located in the fourth galactic quadrant, between Leo and Boötes. The constellation's major stars are Alpha Comae Berenices, Beta Comae Berenices and Gamma Comae Berenices. The constellation's brightest star is Beta Comae Berenices, a 4.2-magnitude main sequence star similar to the Sun. Coma Berenices contains the North Galactic Pole and one of the richest known galaxy clusters, the Coma Cluster, part of the Coma Supercluster.

CHAPTER ONE

I first heard of Apolinar Villa and his contacts in the early 1960s, and obtaining his address at Las Lunas, New Mexico from Gabriel Green, went to see him personally. I found an affable American Indian/Spaniard man, proud of his heritage, married to a German War Bride, Eunis, from his service in our occupation forces after World War Two.

They had moved from Los Angeles, California to New Mexico following the brief publication of his story by Gabriel Green in his *UFO International* journal, with his first set of actual UFO photographs of the alien extraterrestrial vehicles, originally taken with a 120 box camera, then owned by Apolinar and his wife Eunis at the time this all started.

With that story, the UFO fans began looking for Paul Villa for more information and to get copies of his great photographs, the best ever up to that time, for themselves.

The attention bothered Paul so much, and took up so much of his time, that it began to affect his job. He quit that work and moved away, leaving no forwarding address. People who found him, in Albuquerque, New Mexico, took things for souvenirs, which infuriated him, and he took his wife and son and moved again, to an obscure small town in the remote desert south of Albuquerque.

But let us go now to the original *UFO International* report that had caused all this.

THE SECRET UFO CONTACTS OF PAUL VILLA

THE SECRET LIFE OF PAUL VILLA

Most of the saucer photos we have seen previously have been of inferior quality, mainly because the photographer had to grab a shot in a hurry while he had the opportunity.

However, Apolinar (Paul) A. Villa. Jr., 49 (born 24 September 1916), a mechanic by trade, of 601 Niagra, N.E., Albuquerque, New Mexico, holds a unique privilege in the annals of Flying Saucer research. He has had prearranged meetings with space people for the specific purpose of taking pictures of their craft.

Apparently, contacts of one kind or another with the Space People are not new to Mr. Villa. He says that he has been taught telepathically by extraterrestrial intelligences since he was five years old.

Although he did not complete the tenth grade of school, he seems to have a good knowledge of such subjects as mathematics, electricity, Physics, and mechanics, and has an unusual "gift" for detecting defects in engines generators, etc.

Villa says that prior to photographing his first series of saucer pictures in 1963, he had seen about five Flying Saucers in the previous five years, and that he had talked with a spaceman previously. He said that his first picture taking contact was his second in-person meeting with the extraterrestrial beings.

The first was in 1953 while he was working for the Department of Water and Power in Los Angeles. While on the job one day in Long Beach, he had a strong urge to go down to the beach, a feeling he did not then understand. There he met a man about seven feet tall.

At first Villa was afraid of him and wanted to run away. But the man called him by name, and told him many personal things about himself. Villa realized that he was communicating with a very superior intelligence, and he then became aware that this being was a spaceman.

"He knew everything I had in my mind and told me many things that had taken place in my life," Villa says. "He then told me to look out beyond the reef. I saw a metallic-looking disc-shaped object that seemed to be floating on the water. Then the spaceman asked me if I would like to go aboard the craft and look around, and I went with him."

He said the saucer occupants were entirely human looking in appearance, although better looking in general than Earth people, as they were definitely more refined in face and body, also they had an advanced knowledge of science, as evidenced by their craft, and by their talk with him.

They told Villa that the whole Galaxy to which our Earth belongs is as a grain of sand on a huge beach, in relation to the unfathomable number of inhabited galaxies in the entire universe.

Because of their technological advancement, their spaceships can penetrate the Earth's radar detection system, so that they are picked up on our radar detection screens only when they choose to call attention to their presence in our skies. It seems that their craft are constantly active over our surface, and that they plan more sightings and landings in order to increase public awareness of their existence.

They said they were here on a friendly mission to help our people; that they have bases on our Moon; that Phobos, one of the two Moons of Mars is hollow and is artificially constructed; and that there is a Superior Intelligence that governs the Universe and everything in it.

For his first series of pictures (shown in Issue #20 of UFOI), Mr. Villa says that his space contacts told him telepathically, to drive his pickup truck on June 16, (1963), to the meeting place, alone. There he saw a landed saucer which he estimated to be about 70 feet in diameter.

There were 9 people aboard that ship: four men and five women. They disembarked through a hermetically sealed door. These beings, he says, ranged in height from 7 to 9 feet and were all well proportioned. Some were blond; some were red-headed (like polished copper); and some had black hair. They told him they came from the galaxy of Coma Berenices, many light years distant. They were able to speak many languages, as well as to communicate telepathically.

THE SECRET UFO CONTACTS OF PAUL VILLA

UFO INTERNATIONAL

ISSUE NO. 23　　　OCTOBER, 1965　　　50c

THE SECRET UFO CONTACTS OF PAUL VILLA

Amalgamated Flying Saucer Clubs of America
2004 NORTH HOOVER STREET
LOS ANGELES, CALIFORNIA 90027, U.S.A.

Return Requested

Bulk Rate
U. S. POSTAGE
PAID
Los Angeles, Calif.
Permit No. 24309

To:

"UFO INTERNATIONAL" Issue No. 23

AFSCA's PURPOSE: AFSCA is a non-profit organization conducting research and investigation into the subject of flying saucers, interplanetary travel and communication, and related subjects. It endeavors to disseminate the results of such research for the public benefit.

WHAT FLYING SAUCERS ARE: We affirm that flying saucers are real, that they are in reality true spacecraft from other worlds having already accomplished the conquest of space that Earth science hopes to achieve in the next few years. They are manned by people much like ourselves from many other planets, who are visiting and making contact with various persons of our planet for the purpose of imparting vital information, in a gradual manner, which can be used for the benefit of all men of Earth.

SPACE PEOPLE REVEAL SOLUTIONS TO PROBLEMS: It is quite easy for the more advanced people of other planets, having long ago solved the type of problems which seem so insurmountable to men of Earth today, to reveal the solutions which can help the people of Earth in our present time of great crisis. We deplore the actions of our present leaders in withholding information on this subject which is so vital to the health and welfare of our people, our nation, and the world.

NEW SAUCER PHOTOGRAPHS PROVIDE IMPRESSIVE EVIDENCE!

THE SECRET UFO CONTACTS OF PAUL VILLA

Villa was told the craft operated as a mother ship for its nine remotely-controlled monitoring discs which were 14" in diameter, and were controlled from the instrument panels in the mother ship. They could pick up pictures and sounds from any area to which they were directed, and could then relay them back to TV panels aboard the mother craft.

They permitted Villa to take photographs of their ship which they posed and hovered close to the surface between 2:00 and 4:00 P.M. while he took various shots of the craft framed by the trees in the foreground. He used a Japanese-made Rokuoh-Sha camera with an f4.6, 75mm lens, loaded with 120 Kodacolor film. Two of the photos show the ship in a vertical position, on its side, to indicate that the Space People have created an artificial gravity within the craft, and thus are completely comfortable no matter what position the ship is in, relative to a planet's surface.

Incidentally, in photo #7, (seen on page 14 of this book) the vents in the hull, thought by some to be portholes, are not windows, but are openings directly concerned with the propulsion of the ship. Villa says that they told him that the vents are opened only within a planets' atmosphere – never in outer space.

Your editor was formerly a professional photographer, and feels that these pictures are unusually good for several reasons:

1. They are quite sharp, compared to most saucer photos we have seen.

2. The image size of the saucer is large enough to show good detail without extreme graininess.

3. There is a series, instead of just one photo, which provides more details for evaluation.

4. Villa's truck is in the foreground of some of the photos, providing a known object with which to compare the size of the saucer and to judge its distance away.

5. The degree of sharpness of other objects in the near foreground and the clouds and trees in the distance indicates that the object had to be very large in order to achieve the depth of field observed to exist in the photos,

thereby ruling out the possibility that a small model may have been used to fake the photos.

Soon after these photos were released to us, there was a rash of saucer-sighting reports in the newspapers. They began on April 24, 1965 when Socorro, New Mexico, policeman, Lonnie Zamora, saw a landed egg-shaped object take off from a gully and speed away. Soon after this account, other sighting and landing reports came from several western states simultaneously.

So much new interest was stimulated in the saucer subject, that we felt it appropriate to release Mr. Villa's photos to the wire services. Bob Flora, local United Press International photographer, was so impressed with the authentic look of the photos that he put three of them on the UPI wires. They were subsequently printed in hundreds of newspapers throughout the world. The Los Angeles NBC News program also ran the pictures on their color TV newscast for three nights in a row.

As for his second set of pictures, Villa was guided, telepathically again, to another area near Bernalillo, New Mexico - about 15 miles north of Albuquerque. This was on Easter Sunday, April 18, 1965.

The ship seen in photos 1, 2, and 3 projected a ray which caused a small brush fire. The smoke from the fire is visible (more clearly in color) in the trees just below the craft, and just above and to the left of the tailgate of Villa's truck.

In photo number 3 they singed a tree-top – extreme left of the tree grouping - by use of a ray directed from their ship. These things were done to demonstrate some of their capabilities.

The ship landed and Villa judged it to be 300 feet in diameter, it had telescopic, tripod landing gear, which are protruding from the bottom of the craft in photos #1, 2 and 3

The three crewmen (who disembarked) had light brown hair and tan skin. They appeared to be about 5' 8" or 5' 9" tall. Villa talked with them for nearly two hours about personal as well as general matters.

THE SECRET UFO CONTACTS OF PAUL VILLA

They told him that our astronauts, Edward White and James McDivitt, on their now-famous GT-4 flight, were really seeing a spaceship when they reported sighting the Pegasus-like object. They also said that our government won't release the Mariner-4 photos because they show pumping stations for the canal systems on Mars. They added that by 1966, 17 nations will have the Atomic Bomb.

Villa says they conversed both in Spanish (his native language) and in English.

On their advice, the contactee says, he stopped smoking so as to enhance his ability to receive telepathic communications.

Villa said the extraterrestrials he met were entirely human-like in appearance, but better looking in general than Earth people.

THE SECRET UFO CONTACTS OF PAUL VILLA

18 April 1965, 16:00, 20 Miles South of Albuquerque, New Mexico. The branches of the trees in the foreground were being agitated by a strong wind that came up. It shot a beam of light at a bush on the ground and it now burst into flame. It flashed another beam and put the fire out.   Photo #1

18 April 1965, 16:00, 20 Miles South of Albuquerquem New Mexico. The ship made a loud whirring noise and emitted a lot of heat, so hot that it singed the ends of the tree branches on top. The disipating smoke from the bush fire is still seen near the ground in this picture.   Photo #2

THE SECRET UFO CONTACTS OF PAUL VILLA

18 April 1965, 16:00, 20 Miles South of Albuquerque, New Mexico. Apolinar Villa was still being guided telepathically and was near the bend in the Rio Grande River when an immense disc appeared, slowed and hovered about 500 feet above the ground. Photo #3

18 April 1965, 13:30, 10 Miles West of Albuquerque, New Mexico. Apolinar Villa was driving his truck on the road here when a large number of shiny spheres appeared and danced about. After that a huge 100 foot diameter circular craft appeared and took up a vertical position over the desert scrub. Photo #4

THE SECRET UFO CONTACTS OF PAUL VILLA

18 April 1965, 13:30, 10 Miles West of Albuquerque, New Mexico. At times the craft emitted a very high frequency buzz or whine. At other times it was silent. Then the disc started to flip up and down and continued to do so for about 30 seconds and then flew away.

18 April 1965, 13:30, 10 Miles West of Albuquerque, New Mexico. The big ship hovered on edge only a few feet above the desert scrub and slowly turned about a vertical point as Paul Villa watched and snapped a few photographs with his camera.

THE SECRET UFO CONTACTS OF PAUL VILLA

OUR FOLLOW-UP

Jim and Coral Lorenzen, co-founders of APRO (Aerial Phenomena Research Organization) in Tucsom, AZ, reading the report published by Gabriel Green, drove over to Albuquerque to "beard the lion in his den", so to speak. They had the address given in the UFOI article.

They found Paul Villa and his wife Eunis at home and were invited in and offered a glass of tea. As Paul described to me later - Coral started the interview in her usual abrasive manner. Paul told me later, that she propped her elbows on his small dining table, laced her fingers in front of her and started out, "Tell me Paul, just how did you make them?"

By her manner and attitude, Paul assumed that she thought he had faked them, and becoming sarcastic said, "Well, my dear lady, you just make yourself a model and toss it into the air and photograph it." (This is not as easily done as it sounds. I had a lot of difficulty trying to do this myself, and ruined my model by the third picture; and my trying to get them in the correct attitude and angle for the succeeding picture was futile.)

I was hanging around APRO at about that time, and I wrote Paul a letter, apologizing for Coral's crude behavior and asking to come see him. He cordially invited me to do so and I drove over to Albuquerque a few days later to meet the man personally. He was already being badgered by the UFO fans there in Albuquerque as well. They drove over his lawn, backed up and turned around in his garden, took loose articles, and even took his mail out of the mailbox as souvenirs. When they knocked down his yard fence the second time, turning their cars around, he decided he had to move a second time to get away from the public.

He moved his family to Las Lunas, a very small town on the Rio Grande, across the highway from Belen, to a small obscure trailer home there and kept that address secret for his own privacy. It was there that I met him several times and discussed his experiences in great detail.

He mentioned to me that he often stopped at a beer tavern in Belen on his way home from work. One day he came in tired and thirsty and ordered a beer at the bar. As he was sipping it a stranger came up to him and said, "So, you're the nut that is said to be talking to some Spacemen?" and with that he punched Paul on the nose and bloodied him. Paul never forgot that.

Paul was keeping notes on his contacts in spiral bound notebooks, including lengthy discussions with his visitors, who said they came from a star group we catalog as "Coma Berenices" (Latin for Bernices' Comb, a small constellation of stars near Arcturus in the constellation Boötes). The visitors were observing our first attempts at space explorations.

After that Paul Villa called me one morning and invited me back again to tell me about something he did not want to discuss over the telephone.

I flew my little canary yellow American Yankee sport plane over to Kirtland Field at Albuquerque and hired a taxi to drive me to Las Lunas.

When I got there late in the day, Paul stopped what he was doing and sat me down at his kitchen table, brought us both a cup of coffee and sat down across from me.

He said that his friends from space had awakened him at about 02:00 A.M. that morning to tell him about an event that they wanted him to communicate to our own space control people, because they would be very concerned.

Paul told me that his friends from Coma Berenices had awakened him early to tell him that our Mars Probe, then in its final descent phase for landing on Mars, was on a trajectory that would take it over a precipice on Mars and be smashed, and that their attempt to push it back a little to prevent its crash and loss, had upset its gyros which tumbled and caused the craft to somersault just before safe touchdown on its own landing gear. The probe was safely intact and no damage had been suffered, but they thought that our Mission Control would want to know what had happened to the craft, and how it could somersault and still land safely.

Paul went right to work on his telephone to call Houston Control and relay the information. It took him hours to get through to somebody in the control center, and then to talk to a senior Guidance Controller.

When he finally did get somebody in authority there and explained to them what had happened, that controller asked him again who he was and how he got this information. Then asked where he lived and the nearest airport and how to get from the airport to Paul Villa's house. That controller said he would come to Paul to talk to him personally that morning. And he did. He had gone back to Houston by the time I got there.

Paul told me that after listening to all the details and making many notes, that controller confided to Paul personally, that the Mars Lander had indeed somersaulted in its late final descent phase, just before touchdown, as Paul described, but that it landed safely and that the instruments were all working properly.

Before that controller left, he gave Paul Villa a discrete telephone number and asked him to call again whenever he heard from his space friends, which Paul did for a time after that.

Months later I was riding an airliner from San Francisco to Tokyo, and had selected a *TIME* news magazine from the rack. Inside, in the science section, I noticed an article in the middle of the page, outlined with a black border, which described the "impossible" somersault and safe landing on Mars of that probe with no mention of Paul Villa's information. However the article did speculate that the guidance control gyros aboard the craft must have momentarily tumbled for some reason, but reasserted control in time for a safe landing.

When I later saw that same "tumble" in the movie footage in the "Alternative 3" movie, of that landing on Mars, from a camera in the Mars Lander, which showed the horizon "somersaulting" just before the touchdown, my heart leaped into my throat.

When I, sometime after that, in an interview with David Ambrose, one of the authors of the **Alternative 3** book, asked where they got that footage that was shown in the movie version of "Alternative 3," he said he thought they got it from NASA.

Since UFO photographs was "my bag" at that time, I asked Paul Villa a lot of questions about his various photographs of the alien vehicles. He got up, went to a closet, pulled out a big Army foot locker and took out a big brown accordion folder with sets of UFO photographs in it. We took the sets one by one in the order they were taken and examined and discussed them.

THE SECRET UFO CONTACTS OF PAUL VILLA

He gave me copies of two sets I had not seen before, which he said he had not released and asked me not to publish them while he was still alive.

In that folder of photographs were nearly a dozen pictures Paul had shot on another planet that he was taken to by his space friends. This series showed two dinosaur-like beasts, tan and brown splotched in color, with long necks and tails, grazing on the tops of moderate sized trees. One was taking a bite of foliage which he was pulling off the top of one tree while a second one has a mouthful of green from the top of the same tree in his mouth as he turns his head to look at the hovering spacecraft. One can see the rippling muscles and wrinkles in his neck skin where he turned his head. The whole scene, including the other vegetation and sparse grass on a near desert ground was most realistic, and was certainly not a painting. There were three or four of these photographs in close sequence in that series.

He had other sets of photographs that he did not show me at the time, saying that he would give me the whole locker of notes and photographs after he had passed on. He had a growing stomach cancer which I took him to a Philippine healer to treat. The healer said that the condition that caused it still persisted, and that for this reason he could not heal Paul.

The most likely star for the home of these visitors seems to be 12 Coma Berenices, with no NGC number but MEL 111 listing in the MEL catalog, at 250 light years distance and visual magnitude 9 at 12220n2600 coordinates. This Coma group is older than the Pleiades, but younger than the Hyades, according to Burnham's Celestial Handbook Vol. n. Coma Berenices is seen not far from Arcturus and the position of Korendor in the Korena Sun system in the neighboring Constellation Boötes. Whether these two are known to each other, or are simply in the same part of our heavens is simply conjecture, however they both allege that they belong to an Alliance of Planets, and both say that they or their Alliance have bases on our Moon as well as Mars and Venus.

We have few photographs of the Korendian ships, but we do in fact have many photos of the Coma Berenician craft made by Paul Villa over several years of ongoing UFO contact.

The Coma Berenicians, like the Pleiadians visiting "Billy" Meier in Switzerland, actually posed their craft for Paul Villa to get good pictures of

THE SECRET UFO CONTACTS OF PAUL VILLA

them. Many were never released by Paul while he was still alive, because of the attention brought him by the other earlier publications by Gabriel Green. We shall include others in this first release of some of them forever. Paul has now departed from life and we are no longer violating his confidence in doing so.

My only regret is in not being more forceful in getting copies of some of those others, still unreleased, in that folder in Paul's house.

Paul Villa died of that stomach cancer while I was away. His wife Eunis felt so alone without him that she sold the trailer and furnishings and moved away before I got back. I have not been able to find her since. I once got a clue that she had a moved to Green Valley, here south of Tucson, to stay with her a sister who had moved here also, but I have never found the name of that married sister and Eunis Villa is not listed in any of the records systems here under that name.

It is difficult to ascertain where exactly Paul Villa's visitors may originate. The Coma Berenices constellation, as seen from Earth, contains about 100 stars in the Coma star cluster. This cluster, which is within our Milky Way Galaxy, is some 288 light-years distant. However, the Coma Cluster, a group of galaxies, can also been seen beyond Coma Berenices. These galaxies extend far into interstellar space. How many suns and how many worlds might be located in this direction of space?

THE SECRET UFO CONTACTS OF PAUL VILLA

I would love to find Eunis and that metal bound military foot locker full of contact notes, objects and things that Paul had collected on his contacts with the Coma Berenicians.

But let us now go to the UFO photographs taken by Paul Villa that we do still have in our files.

PHOTOGRAPHIC FOLDERS

I have liberally borrowed the following three folders of Paul Villa UFO photographs from my "***UFO PHOTOGRAPHS AROUND THE WORLD***," Vol. 4, which already covered them in as much detail as we have to date. It is in that volume that we covered Mini-UFOs around the world, starting with a case in Sweden and covering all the mini UFOs photographed by Paul Villa.

Those folders follow.

THE ALBUQUERQUE PHOTOGRAPHS

The extended experiences of long term UFO contactees casts new light on one of those domestic cases which began over 15 years ago. Like the photographs by Harold Trudel, Howard Menger, George Adamski and others, these UFO photos have been condemned by the UFO clubs and the usual detractors without the benefit of any proper analysis or testing of any kind. The condemnation was always proclaimed, without substantiation, by subjective deduction on the part of the self styled "experts" purely on the basis of their expert knowledge of the subject area. No laboratory testing or analysis of the original image was ever accomplished; no efforts to duplicate the pictures that they say could be so easily duplicated was ever undertaken, and no equivalent photographs have been artificially produced up to this time by anyone. We submit that these series of photographs need more study and analysis in the light of present technology.

Like some of the other pictures mentioned, those made by Apolinar Villa were considered to be "too well posed," whatever that means, and showed the details of these peculiar structured objects too well for

THE SECRET UFO CONTACTS OF PAUL VILLA

comparison with the rest of the UFO photographs available. They looked posed, and we later found out that they actually were posed by the occupants aboard, according to their own statements.

Like Eduard Meier of Switzerland, Paul Villa was persecuted by almost everyone, including even his neighbors, perhaps in envy because the experience had happened to him instead of them, a position also taken by many UFO researchers.

The fact remains, however, as in Meier's case, that the spacecraft were actually posed for photographs in some of these cases for reasons unknown to us. Also in roost extensive on-going UFO contact cases we have noted that a variety of spacecraft are used by the same group for different purposes, a situation not too difficult to understand. In all of these cases mentioned, at least three different types of craft, in different sizes, were used.

If we accept the debunker's hypothesis that the ships were carefully constructed models, cleverly posed and photographed as deliberate hoaxes, why build so many different types and sizes; and whatever happened to the models? A variety of models and sizes seriously aggravates the problems of secrecy and avoiding discovery for all these years. None of these men had extra money or resources available to spend on jokes, and none of them ever made any money on his experiences. On the contrary, all were harassed and threatened, and were forced to move for their own and their family's safety, certainly no experience deliberately sought by any of them. And besides that, after their misfortune with their first pictures, one would think they would have little desire to continue building and photographing more models. As a matter of fact, all of than have taken more photographs still, which have never been released, and may never be. None of them need proof of the reality of their experiences by comparing them with others, because they have their own proof all the time. They do not care at this point whether anyone else believes them or not.

As with several others, Paul Villa's contacts with the space people were not new to him by the time he snapped the first photographs. He says that he has been taught telepathically by extraterrestrial intelligences since he was five years old...about the same as with Eduard Meier. Although he did not complete the 10th grade in public school, he has an excellent knowledge of

THE SECRET UFO CONTACTS OF PAUL VILLA

most subjects – including mathematics, electrical engineering, physics, mechanics, etc., which also agrees remarkably well with the background of some of the other contactees.

Prior to photographing his first UFO in 1963, Villa had seen about five spacecraft over the previous five years and had even conversed with spacemen previously. His first picture-taking contact was his second in-person face-to-face meeting with the extraterrestrial beings who told him they came from a planet in the star-group we call Coma Berenices. The first was in 1953 while he was working for the Department of Water and Power in Los Angeles.

While on a job one day in the Long Beach area, he felt a strong urge to go down to the beach, a feeling which he did not understand, but he went anyway. There he met a man about seven feet tall. At first he was afraid and just wanted to run, but the man called him by name and told him many personal things about himself. Villa realized that he was communicating with a very superior intelligence, and he then became aware that this being was a spaceman.

"He knew everything I had in my mind and told me many things that had taken place in my life," Villa says. "He then told me to look out beyond the reef. I did and saw a metallic-looking disc-shaped craft that seemed to be floating on the water. Then the spaceman asked me if I would like to go aboard the ship and look around, and I went with him.

"The beings on the craft were entirely human-like in appearance, although better looking in general than our Earth people, as they were definitely more refined in face and form. Also they had an advanced knowledge of science and technology, as evidenced by their craft, and by their conversation with me."

Those beings told Villa that the whole Galaxy to which our Earth belongs is as a grain of sand on a huge beach compared to the unfathomable number of inhabited bodies in the entire Universe.

With technological equipment aboard, their spaceships can penetrate Earth's RADAR detection systems undetected unless they choose otherwise.

THE SECRET UFO CONTACTS OF PAUL VILLA

It seems that their craft are constantly active over the surface of our planet, and that they plan more landings.

They told Villa that they were here on a friendly mission to help Earth people, and that there is a superior intelligence that governs the Universe and everything in it.

The first series of photographs of these ships, taken on 16 June 1963, was prompted Villa says, when the space contacts told him telepathically to drive his pick-up truck to a preselected meeting place alone. When he arrived, he saw a landed spacecraft which he estimated to be about 70 feet in diameter. There were nine people aboard that ship; four men and five women; they disembarked through a "sealed" door (that couldn't be seen when closed). These beings ranged in height from seven to nine feet tall and were well proportioned. Some were blond, some were red-headed (like polished copper), and some had black hair. They told him they came from a planet near what we call Coma Berenices, some light years distant. They were able to speak many languages, as well as to communicate telepathically among themselves and to him.

Villa was told that this ship carried nine remotely-controlled monitoring craft which were about 14" in diameter, and were controlled from instrument panels within the mother-ship. They could pick up pictures and sounds from any area to which the instruments were directed, and could relay information to visual display panels aboard the larger ship.

After a long conversation the space people re-entered their spaceship and it took off and hovered and maneuvered about the area for some time. At one point it hovered about 300 feet above the pickup truck and Villa saw it rise slowly from the ground to a height of three or four feet and then slowly settle back down again. The spacecraft then flipped up on its edge with the under part rotating, and traveled sidewise up and down at different speeds. The distortion on the leading edge of the craft in photo number three is caused by the rotation of the lower half of the ship and the swaying branches of the trees which were put into motion by a big rush of wind.

Villa took seven photographs at this time...this was all that was left on the roll of film, before the ship departed.

THE SECRET UFO CONTACTS OF PAUL VILLA

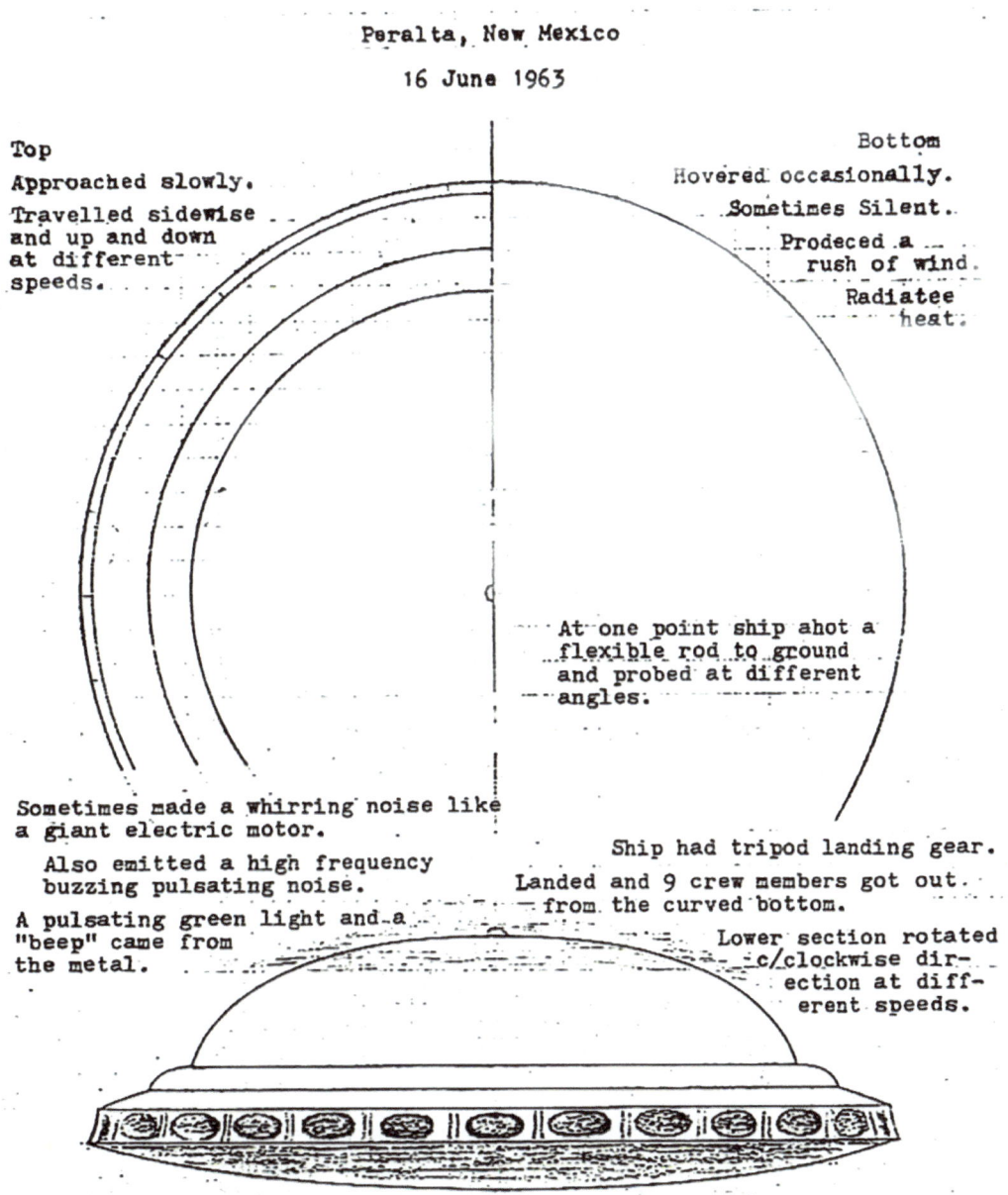

16 June 1963, 14:00-16:00, Peralta, New Mexico. Line Drawing of the spacecraft whose occupants told Paul Villa they came from a place in the heavens which we call Coma Berenices. He took pictures of their ship after they took off. They hovered it in demonstration for him.

THE SECRET UFO CONTACTS OF PAUL VILLA

16 June 1963, 15:30, Peralta, New Mexico. Photographs numbers 1 and 2 above show the slow reapproach of the alien spacecraft after a quick departure following a conversation on the ground with the ET occupants aboard.

THE SECRET UFO CONTACTS OF PAUL VILLA

16 June 1963, 15:30, Peralta, New Mexico. Photos number 3 and 4 show the continuation of the demonstration approach now descending to near tree top level. The tree branches were put in motion by a big rush of wind from the ship.

THE SECRET UFO CONTACTS OF PAUL VILLA

In photo number five the spaceship is seen between tree trunks. It hovered in that vicinity for some time. The "ports" around the outer edge of the rim are a part of the propulsion system. No jets or rockets of any kind are employed. The "ports" are never used or left unsealed outside the planet's atmosphere where the magnetic lines of force are further apart, but are hermetically sealed either manually or automatically before leaving a planetary atmosphere. Hermetic sealing is accomplished by removing all foreign substances from the basic elements of the parent metals, and a device is used to charge both surfaces to be sealed either positively or negatively, depending on how a certain metal is naturally charged. The sealing of two or more metals cannot be accomplished unless they are first neutralized and then are all charged with the same polarity. The carbon elements, however, being anphoteric combine equally well with positively or negatively charged elements.

When Villa arrived on the scene of this encounter, the spacecraft was resting on the ground on its tripod landing gear, and the nine crew members immediately disembarked from under the disc-shaped bottom of the craft through a door that seemed to appear from nowhere.

All of the beings were dressed alike in immaculate one-piece tight-fitting uniforms. They acted very friendly, and seemed to be aware of and to have answers to many of Earth's problems. They talked to Villa for about ninety minutes, from around 14:30 to 16:00. When talking to Mr. Villa they spoke in both English and Spanish languages, mostly Spanish. But when conversing among themselves they used their own language, which sounded a little like Hebrew or Indian.

Some of the crew members carried "weapons" that looked like ordinary tubes made of aluminum about eight inches long and one inch in diameter, tapering slightly from the center outwards. These, they said, could paralyze any living thing, whether insect, fowl, animal or man. They looked like tubes used for "sealing" metals, only in miniature.

While inside the ship, Villa noticed a pulsating green light accompanied by a sort of "beep." Both the green light and the noise seemed to come right from the metal of the ship itself.

THE SECRET UFO CONTACTS OF PAUL VILLA

The Coma Berenicians expressed a wish for Earth people to rise above their aggressive and warlike inclinations and live in harmony with the Universal Laws of the great Creator, as do the people of other worlds, they said that LOVE is the most powerful force in the Universe, and that if used correctly, can transform the hearts of men and make them into beings of light and peace. When the law of LOVE rules the minds of men of Earth, then the people of other worlds will come in great numbers and share with us their advanced sciences, living among us as friends and brothers in lasting peace, as they do on many other worlds.

Paul Villa's photographs are unique for a number of reasons:

1. They are quite sharp and clear, compared to most UFO photos we have seen up to that time.

2. The image size of the UFO is large enough to show detail without getting into extreme graininess in large scale enlargements.

3. There is a series instead of just one photograph under very poor conditions, a series which provides more detail for evaluation, and provides more opportunity for discovery of possible suspension lines or other photo trickery.

4. Villa's truck in the foreground of several of the pictures provides a known object with which to compare size, light scatter, shadows, relative proportions, etc., as well as providing a reference for distance.

5. The degree of sharpness of other objects in the near foreground and the clouds and trees in the distance indicates that the object had to be very large in order to achieve the depth of field observed to exist in these photographs, which operates against the small model hypothesis.

Mr. Gabriel Green of AFSCA, a professional photographer himself who once worked for MGM studios, took the first set of pictures to MGM laboratories where they blew them up in progressive stages to control graininess, to 30 by 50 inches for the UK image alone, and printed then in light and dark, high and low contrast, and by a process called "slow-bum" (using narrower aperture and longer time), looking for suspension lines and fine detail. Now after days of laboratory effort, they concluded that if those pictures were faked they did not know how it could be done.

THE SECRET UFO CONTACTS OF PAUL VILLA

Mr. Bob Flora, a United Press International photographer, was so impressed with the authentic look of these pictures that he put three of them on the UPI wires and they were subsequently printed in hundreds of newspapers all over the world. The Los Angeles NBC Ness program broadcast these pictures on their new color TV newscast for three nights in a row.

But the most important thing is that this was not an isolated instance. The contacts continued for a good many years until Paul Villa' s death in September of 1982 in Las Lunas, New Mexico. Mr. Villa has taken many more photographs of the spaceships of his friends and, to his regret, even released more of them to friends promising to observe his confidence. Some of these new pictures got out and were subsequently published, adding to the woes of his harassment. He has become so bitter about the treatment such a person gets that he had moved to a secluded location and kept an unlisted telephone number known to only a very few friends. In later life he refused to show or even discuss the pictures with any but his closest friends, who, knowing the problems involved, respected his confidence and his privacy. There was no need to go looking for him because he kept himself very difficult to find, and if found, would very likely refuse to discuss the pictures. He was just not at all interested in what others thought. It had no bearing cm the truths he knew first hand.

Paul Villa's second set of UFO photographs was also taken coincident with a face-to-face meeting with the UFOnauts on the ground. This time he was telepathically directed to a different area, about 20 miles due south of Albuquerque, close to the bed of the Rio Grande River which flows there, when an immense disc-shaped craft appeared. It was Easter Sunday the 18th of April 1965, and about 16:00 in the afternoon when he arrived on scene.

This ship looked to be considerably more than 100 feet in diameter. The big ship slowed and hovered about 500 feet above him. He began snapping pictures. A wind disturbance arose and became so strong that at one point Villa thought his truck might blow over. Then without warning, it suddenly stopped, just as though someone had turned it off, and the surrounding air got warm and there was dead silence. Then the huge ship extended a telescopic tripod landing gear and settled on it, part of which may be seen in one of the photos.

THE SECRET UFO CONTACTS OF PAUL VILLA

This time three crewmen disembarked. They had light brown hair and tan skin, and appeared to be 5' 8" to 5' 9" tall. They also wore one-piece suits. Villa talked to them there for nearly two hours about personal as well as general subjects. Among other things, they told him that many nations were working on atom bombs. They also conversed in both Spanish and English. On their advice, Villa stopped smoking so as to enhance his ability to receive their telepathic communications. The men then re-entered the spacecraft and it took off, making a loud whirring noise and giving off much heat. The heat became so intense that the ends of the tree branches were singed and the leaves curled up.

Villa snapped pictures of the big ship both before and after the landing but did not attempt to take pictures of either the ship on the ground or of the occupants because he had been asked not to do so both telepathically and verbally on the ground, and he willingly complied with their wishes.

Paul Villa sought no personal publicity and did not lecture or sell any of his pictures or accounts of the UFO contacts. The contacts continued and more pictures were taken. The additional information and other photos, Villa insisted, were not to be released without his prior permission by the space people, and to his death he observed that later prohibition.

Villa made many noted about his contacts and the dialogues which took place with the extraterrestrials, a collection of notes which exceeded 800 pages last time I saw them. He refused to let them be quoted or published while he was alive. His wife Eunice has them new and may agree at some time in the future to allow then to be published.

Paul Villa's excellent photographs have made such an impression that opposing forces frequently try to discredit then. They are quick to pronounce them fakes but at the same time they offer no substantive proof to back up these allegations. The fact remains however, that all those trying to discredit them, and unbelievable measures have been taken to do so, have failed to find any models or accomplices, or any real evidence of fraud, and nobody to this day has been able to duplicate than. Either those opponents have to be wrong or Paul Villa was the best photographic effects man in the world and he wasn't even a photo hobbyist.

THE SECRET UFO CONTACTS OF PAUL VILLA

For those technical experts interested, Mr. Villa used a Japanese Rokuoh-Sha camera with an f.4.5, 75rrcn focal length lens. The pictures were all made on Kodacolor 120 size film without filters or lens attachments.

All of Villa's UFO photographs were taken with an inexpensive Rokuoh-Sha camera.

THE SECRET UFO CONTACTS OF PAUL VILLA

PERALTA, NEW MEXICO - 16 June 1963, 14:00-16:00

Mr. Paul Villa, upon impulse, drove his pick-up truck to a designated place along the Rio Grande River fifteen miles south of Albuquerque, near the town of Peralta. When he arrived, he found a landed circular craft about 70 feet in diameter resting on tripod landing gear. As soon as he arrived, a port opened from nowhere in the bottom of the ship and nine human-like beings disembarked, four men and five women and stood on the ground to meet him.

They came out of the ship through a sealed door that he did not see when he drove up. These were big people seven to nine feet tall and well proportioned. Some were blond, some had reddish hair and some had black hair. They told the witness that they came from a planet in another system in a place we call Coma Berencies, many light years distant. They spoke to him in English and Spanish and also communicated telepathically. They spoke to each other in another language he did not understand.

The visitors told Villa they had nine remotely controlled discs aboard. They were about 14" in diameter and were controlled from instrument panels in the mother ship. These discs could pick up pictures and sounds from any place they were sent to and could relay data back to the big ship instantly.

After a long conversation the ship took off and put on a hovering and maneuvering aerial demonstration for the witness as he took a series of seven color photographs, all of the film left on the roll in the camera.

At one point it hovered about 300 feet above the pickup truck and raised it slowly to a height of three to four feet and then, as it hung there, a small whirlwind formed and went all around under the suspended truck as it slowly turned around 180 degrees to head the opposite way. Then it slowly settled on the ground again. Villa asked what the whirlwind was and was told that it was to remove the small creatures on the ground from danger before they set the truck back down, a remarkable demonstration of thoughtfulness that Villa never forgot.

At one point the big craft flipped up on its edge, the under part visibly rotating, and moved sidewise up and down at different speeds. A Visible distortion on the leading edge of the craft in photo number three is caused by the rotation of the lower part of the ship and the swaying of the tree branches which were put into motion by a big rush of wind.

In photo number five the spaceship is seen between tree trunks. It hovered in this vicinity for some time. The "ports" on the outer edge of the rim are part of the propulsion system. No jets or rockets are employed. The "ports" are sealed outside a planet's atmosphere.

The ship was about a quarter of a mile away when photo number 6 was snapped. It shot something down toward the ground that looked like a big hose, but at closer range was seen to be a flexible controlled rod, probing the ground and trees at different angles, and curving into different shapes.

While this was going on, a small shiny silver sphere about 6 feet in diameter came out of the ship and descended to the ground and disappeared behind the trees. What its purpose was or what it did is not known, but when it reappeared it shot at terrific speed to the northwest and disappeared. When this sphere descended from the ship it had a shiny chrome appearance, but when it sped away it turned a kind of reddish color.

Photo number seven shows the ship beyond the treetops and several hundred yards away, the bottom of the disc became tinted an amber red, like hot metal, but would also change in finish from shiny chrome to a dull aluminum appearance and back to bright red again. At one time it became so intensely bright that its brilliance shown like the sun and it was blinding to look at. It passed over Mr. Villa's head and he could feel the heat and a prickling sensation all over his body.

Although the upper domed section can be turned independently from the lower section, it appeared to remain stationary during flight while the lower section rotated at different speeds.

It made a whirring noise which sounded something like a giant electric motor or generator in operation. Then at other times it would give off a buzzing, pulsating noise, or suddenly become absolutely silent as it continued to move about in different directions.

From extensive interviews with Paul Villa.

THE SECRET UFO CONTACTS OF PAUL VILLA

16 June 1963, 15:30, Peralta, New Mexico. Photos number 5 and 6 show the closest approach of the ship during the picture taking. Note the corona of ionized vapor around the crown of the dome of this big ship. After photo number 6 it shot something down toward the ground.

THE SECRET UFO CONTACTS OF PAUL VILLA

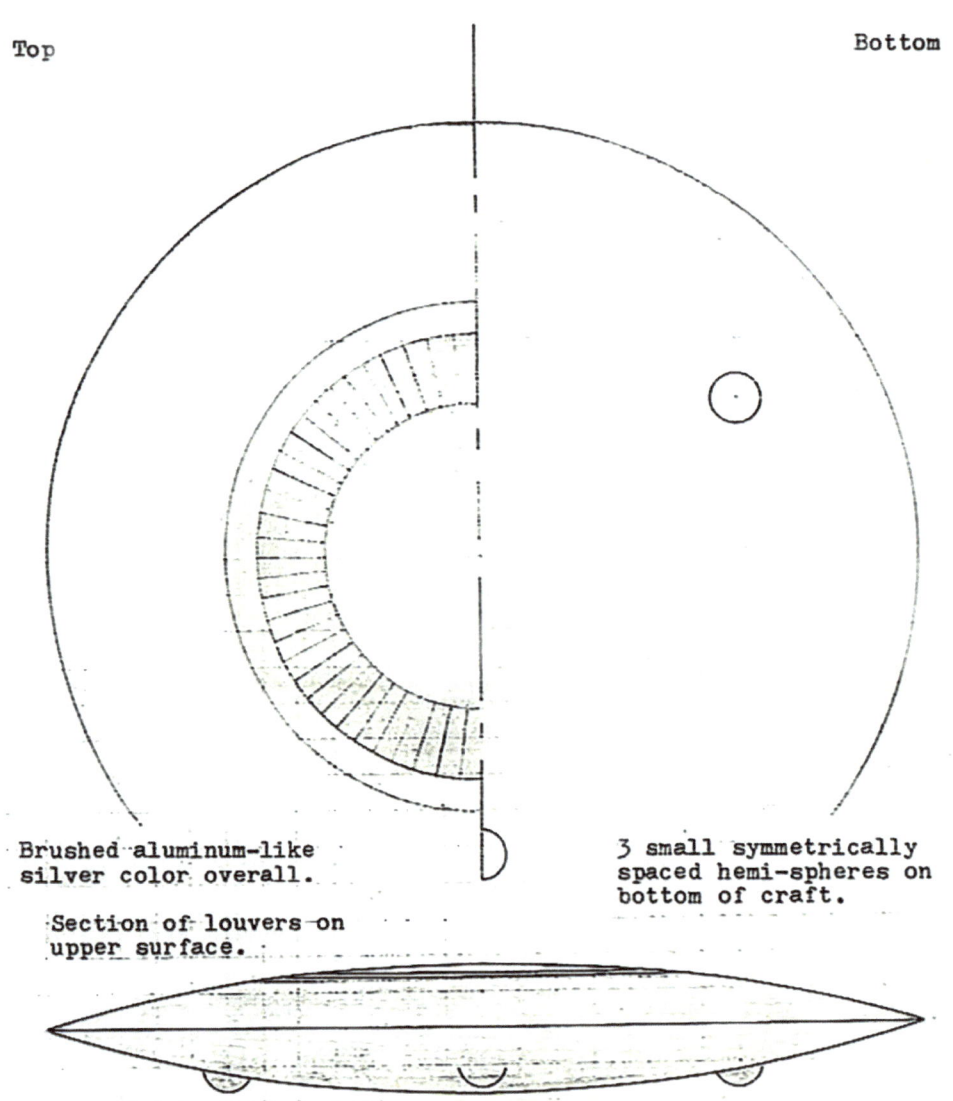

18 April 1965, 13:30, 10 miles west of Albuquerque, New Mexico. After first seeing a number of flying shiny spheres, this big disc-shaped craft appeared and hovered on edge just above the desert scrub. This line drawing is made from the photos and Villa's personal description.

THE SECRET UFO CONTACTS OF PAUL VILLA

BERNALILLO, NEW MEXICO - 18 April 1965, 09:00

On Easter Sunday, 18 April 1965, Apolinar Villa was again guided telepathically, to a different area, near Bernalillo, about 15 miles north of Albuquerque. At near 09:00 A.M., as he was some five miles southwest of Sandia Indian Pueblo, he spotted a craft hovering silently in the air above. He stopped and got out and snapped one photograph of it, and then waited to see what it was going to do.

After about 10 minutes it suddenly shot straight up and made an abrupt' 90 degree change of direction and it quickly disappeared heading due north. He did not get another picture before it was gone.

An hour later, not too far from the same location, he saw a craft again. As before, it was hovering silently above but he noticed an air turbulence swirling around under it. He took another picture, this time at an angle showing an ellipse, but the object was identical to the one seen earlier.

18 April 1965, 09:00, Bernalillo, New Mexico. The craft slowly moved about overhead and Paul Villa snapped this second photograph of the object above some trash and debris there. Note the distance graying of ship.

THE SECRET UFO CONTACTS OF PAUL VILLA

10 MILES WEST OF ALBUQUERQUE, NEW MEXICO
18 April 1965, 13:30

At about 13:30 in the afternoon, Apolinar Villa was driving his truck about 10 miles west of Albuquerque, as a large number of mirror-bright shiny silver spheres of different sizes ranging from one to an estimated 15 feet in diameter, appeared and flitted and danced about in the sky as they left visible trails creating astounding cloud patterns. After the fast-moving spheres had completed this remarkable display, a huge circular craft, estimated to be over 100 feet in diameter, appeared and took up a position hovering in the air on edge only a few dozen feet above the desert scrub and about a half mile to a quarter of a mile away. It slowly turned about a vertical point, and the witness noticed what looked like three small hemispherical structures of some kind on the surface nearest him. They were arranged symmetrically near the center and may have been some kind of landing gear.

At times, as the craft moved into different positions, it emitted a very high frequency buzz or whine. At other times it was completely silent. He snapped pictures No. 3, 4, and 5 on that roll of film. Photo No. 4 was taken about two minutes after No. 3. The ship had moved into edgewise position in line with the camera and resembled a thin double convex lens. Photo No. 5 was taken a few minutes after No. 4 as the disc started flipping up and down, and continued to do so for about 30 seconds. Then the spacecraft resumed its steady attitude and the many shiny spheres that had first appeared entered into it in some unseen way and the craft shot off at terrific speed and disappeared in a northwesterly direction.

8 MILES NORTH OF ALBUQUERQUE, NEW MEXICO
18 April 1965, 14:00

At about 14:00 on 18 April, 1965, as Apolinar Villa was about eight miles north of Albuquerque, between the Rio Grande River and Sandia Mountain Range; he saw another disc-shaped craft. This one was more distant and Villa did not get close enough to estimate its size, but it was much like the big lens-shaped craft seen earlier and may even have been the same one. It was visible for only a few seconds and then it shot over the Sandia Mountains seen in the background and was gone. He managed to snap picture number 6 on the film roll of this object.

20 MILES SOUTH OF ALBUQUERQUE, NEW MEXICO
18 April 1965, 16:00

By 16:00 that same Easter Sunday, Apolinar Villa was still being telepathically guided around, and was then some 20 miles south of Albuquerque, close to the bend in the Rio Grande River. Suddenly an immense disc-shaped craft appeared. He estimated this one to be considerably more than 100 feet in diameter. It slowed and hovered about 500 feet above the surface. He snapped pictures No. 7 and 8 on the roll of film in his camera.

The branches of the trees in the foreground are blurry because they were being agitated by a strong wind disturbance created by the craft. The wind disturbance got so high in the area that Villa thought he and his truck might be blown over. Then without warning, the wind suddenly stepped, instantly, just as though someone had turned it off, and the surrounding air became warm and there was dead silence. Then the huge ship descended and landed on telescopic tripod legs, part of which may be seen protruding from the ship in one of the photos.

Three crewmen about 5' 8" to 5' 9" tall and wearing one- piece close-fitting suits got out of the craft and spoke with Villa for over an hour. They conversed in both English and Spanish. The visitors advised Villa to stop his smoking habit so as to enhance his ability to receive their telepathic communications. The men reentered the ship and it took off, making a loud whirring noise and giving out much heat. The heat became so intense that it burnt the ends of the tree branches.

Villa snapped photo No. 9, showing the craft high above and to the left of the truck's tailgate seen in the foreground of the picture. That picture shows a tiny cloud of smoke on the ground. The spacecraft had shot a bright beam of light at the ground causing the brush and trees to burst into flame. It shot another beam of light and the fire was instantly extinguished. The spaceship sped away in a northeasterly direction.

THE SECRET UFO CONTACTS OF PAUL VILLA

18 April 1965, 14:00, 8 Miles North of Albuquerque, New Mexico. Apolinar Villa was 8 miles north of Albuquerque, between the Rio Grande River and the Sandia Mountain Range when he saw another large disc-shaped craft hovering on edge over the desert scrub.

18 April 1965, 16:00, 20 Miles South of Albuquerque, New Mexico. The branches of the trees in the foreground were being agitated by a strong wind that came up. It shot a beam of light at a bush on the ground and it now burst into flame. It flashed another beam and put the fire out.

THE SECRET UFO CONTACTS OF PAUL VILLA

MINI-UFOS

Although the subject of Mini-UFOs sounds quite exotic within the already rarified field of UFO research, there is really a considerable amount of information on them for anyone who wants to undertake the necessary research.

This is a good place to introduce this subject because the last three series of UFO photographs taken by Paul Villa included such small flying objects. But these were not the first nor the only observations or photographs of these diminutive craft – Indeed, there are a great many cases of mini-UFOs reported –and mini-occupants too – enough to fill a good sized book, and so we will limit our coverage to outlining a few representative cases, mostly involving photographs of the miniatures, in keeping with the theme of this book.

Among the first mini-UFOs reported in available literature is the small flying object observed and photographed at Aalborg, Denmark on 29 January 1963. It was about 15:15 in the afternoon when Christian Lynggaard watched a small 3" to 5" diameter transparent sphere, like a soap bubble, which at times looked transparent and at other times seemed to be more metallic as it moved along the city street, showing all the signs of intelligent control. It was traveling just above street level and seemed to be inspecting automobiles parked at the curb. After watching it for a few moments Christian got his camera and followed it snapping pictures as it proceeded along, until he finished the roll of film in his camera.

The next set of pictures of these small round objects was made two years later, on 18 April 1965 at a point 10 miles west of Albuquerque by Apolinar Villa as the tiny round objects flew all about over the desert area there leaving visible trails that developed into cloud patterns of interesting shapes. These mirror-bright shiny spheres ranged in size from 3" up to three and six feet, and went from shiny opaque metallic to dull finish reflective metallic and also became radiantly luminous at times, and going through all the hues of heating metal to incandescent reds, oranges, yellows and even blues and greens. They emitted buzzing sounds that changed with the color changes and speeds. The manner of flight was fast and slow with abrupt changes of direction.

THE SECRET UFO CONTACTS OF PAUL VILLA

19 January 1963, 15:15, Aalborg, Denmark. Mr. Christian Lynggaard, walking along a street in Aalborg, saw some very strange and highly persistent "soap Bubbles" floating along as though they were under intelligent control. He opened his camera and started taking pictures of the phenomenon.

19 January 1963, 15:15, Aalborg, Denmark. Mr. Christian Lynggaard, watching the small round transparent and quite persistent "bubbles", thought they seemed to be under intelligent control as they purposefully moved along a line of parked cars as though inspecting them.

THE SECRET UFO CONTACTS OF PAUL VILLA

Fourteen months after that, on 19 June 1966, Apolinar Villa again encountered the mini-UFOs launched by the big discs from Coma Berenices. He had seen them several more times since the April 1965 event, but this time he had his camera with him again and was able to get more and better pictures of the mirror spheres.

It was about 09:00 as he was near Algondones, New Mexico, north of Albuquerque, when the shiny flying balls appeared in a clear blue sky. This time they were accompanied by several small silvery discs of three to six feet in diameter which seemed to be remotely controlled too. The spheres sometimes joined the discs and flew rapid orbits around them at high speed, changing color, radiance, and sound intensity at the same time. These spheres were in a number of sizes this time, but only the small ones of a few inches to a few feet came down low enough to be observed. But this was not all. Villa would see the tiny flying objects again.

On the 24th of July 1966, at Woonsocket, Rhode Island, Harold Trudel photographed two silvery metallic flying discs before the very eyes of the UFO field investigator examining the site of an earlier report of observation and photographs by the same witness. The first lens-like mini-disc, between two and three feet in diameter came down at a steep angle from the right and was spotted by Joseph L. Ferriere who yelled for Trudel to "Come here, quick!"

As Trudel ran forward another identical tiny disc-shaped flying object sped down from the left and the two craft met at about the height of the power lines there where one of them made a very tight loop around the power lines and they swooped back up steeply into the sky and disappeared. Trudel managed to snap two photographs of this spectacular demonstration.

At the Highwood Ranger Station, 50 miles southwest of Calgary, Alberta, Warren Smith and two companions saw a small dark round flying object cane out of a much larger double domed flying disc and go down behind some trees to where they could not see it any longer. That was at about 17:30 Pacific Standard Time on 3 July 1967, one of the biggest years for UFO activity. The small spherical object was only inches in diameter and the mother-ship had a smooth metallic finish and was estimated to be about 25 feet across.

THE SECRET UFO CONTACTS OF PAUL VILLA

19 June 1966, 09:00, Algondones, New Mexico. As Apolinar Villa was about 3 miles west of Algondones, he saw a small "flock" of shiny spheres and silvery metallic flying discs of quite small size flitting along over the desert scrub there. He got out his camera and started taking pictures of them.

19 January 1966, 09:00, Algondones, New Mexico. Then one of the silvery discs approached and Paul Villa tried to get it in the picture with one of the small shiny spheres, and succeeded in doing so. There were also some larger spheres higher up that did not come down to his level.

THE SECRET UFO CONTACTS OF PAUL VILLA

On 12 March 1968, during the early night hours, Sr. J.A. Romando of Moreno, Argentina, filmed 8mm movies of a thick circular flying object shaped like an inverted bowl as it "gave birth to a round radiant ball of bright light which then separated from the larger craft and then flew away independently.

On 17 May 1968, at Gaconde, near Botucatu, SP, Brazil, Sr. Caetano Sergio dos Santos arrived home from his night work, at about 05:00 A.M., and discovered, to the right of the outside door to his home, a short and fat metallic cylinder about 17 centimeters long by 15 in diameter, which he lightly kicked with his toe. He then reached down to pick it up and found it too heavy to move with one hand, and thought that it deceptively had the weight of a much larger object. He felt it might be mostly solid metal like an automobile generator. His curiosity aroused, he bent down and using both hands picked it up and examined it. Its surface was of gray metal, smooth, solid. He couldn't pry it open with a screwdriver nor could he puncture a hole in either the metal of the transparent panels that covered the clocklike arched scales in the two ends of the cylinder. The scales were marked in strange symbols and ended in a dot at one side. A black needle swept the scale. Both ends of the cylinder were the same but the symbols were different. After examining it for about a half hour the witness set it down inside the house and went to bed.

The next morning, as he was outside eating an orange, he remembered the object and went to look at it again to see if the airplane had any effect on the pointer that swept the scale. The pointer had not moved. He threw the object violently to the ground trying to provoke some movement of the pointers, which meanwhile had moved away from the dot at the end of the scale. Giving up, he put it out of reach of the children between an oil lamp and two chunks of soap on top of the cistern in the wall of the kitchen.

That night, as he left for work, about thirty minutes after midnight, he looked at the object and noticed a strange luminance in the lamplight. At 01:07 he heard that his wife had called for help from a neighbor and he ran home. There he found his wife sitting on the porch, in her nightgown holding the children. He was able to understand from his wife that only a few minutes before, all had been treated to a spectacle for some 15 to 20 minutes inside his house, which she was forced to leave with her children. She had heard a loud buzz that came from the direction of the kitchen, from where there also emanated a bright bluish light, which she could easily see because the house had no interior finishing. She also felt a strange heat within the heat of the house. Suddenly the electric lights went out and she thought of the circuit breaker, but the heat was increasing, so she grabbed the two children out of their beds and ran out of the house into the cold night. They were all crying and she shouted to her neighbors for help.

Suddenly there was a strange noise in the roof tiles in the kitchen, from where they saw pieces of tile showering down. After this all became very quiet. The bluish light and the buzzing noise were gone from inside the house, and that was about the time that Caetano ran up to them. The husband went into the house to investigate and found the object gone from on top of the cistern. The roof tiles above the cistern box now had a hole completely through and broken tile lay all around. He went to get the authorities.

In August 1968, after a prolonged build-up over many months, luminous flying objects that had been plaguing the Wilson Gusmao farm returned in force. On the 17th they carried out extensive operations over the property, stopping the truck and blacking out the power although the diesel power generator continued to run. Wilson had alerted the authorities before, and now he was joined at his farm by General Moacir Oschoa, Major Jacob Zweiter, and an official party of scientists, who observed the phenomenon personally and left instructions to be kept advised.

On 31 January 1969, General Oschoa arrived again with his team to observe a now almost nightly approach by the flying object. At about 20:00 a UPO appeared and went through the customary maneuvering ritual, and then came up to within 20 meters of the group of investigators in front of the house, passed along the line of cars and descended to a brushy flat on a hill 100 meters from the group. Photographer Luiz Albuquerque accompanying the team snapped several pictures of the glowing object as it flew above the trees.

Wilson Gusmao went up to within one meter of this glowing object hovering there, and saw that it was an obviously controlled ship of small size, about one meter wide by two meters long with a beacon of light in front. As he watched, a little port opened in the side on top of the thing and a tiny human-like being came out and stood in the air, levitated in space above the ground.

THE SECRET UFO CONTACTS OF PAUL VILLA

The little ship balanced itself in the air a half meter above the ground as Albuquerque snapped a second and third photo of this phase of the event. The little UFOnaut looked steadily at Wilson, then at a box at the beltline of his suit. Wilson followed his gaze and then the UFOnaut moved his hand and pressed a button on the box, giving Wilson the impression that he was being photographed. A blue light came from the box and then went out. The UFOnaut then turned his back to Wilson and looked into his tiny ship.

Suddenly there was a great light on the hill behind the farmhouse and a huge ship rose up radiating a resplendent, brilliant light in all directions in perfect view of all the witnesses. Following that the little man turned around again and faced Wilson, then looked at the group of witnesses watching intently, some with binoculars, kind of smiled at Wilson and lifted his hand to another button on his belt which, when pressed, produced a luminous halo or mass of dense light around him. Now the other witnesses could only see Wilson and the bright ball of light, which Jose Albuquerque also photographed.

The little UFOnaut made a simple sign to Wilson, like a salute, and reentered the tiny ship with his legs held forward as he had come out, and the port closed behind him. The little ship ascended and disappeared into the bigger one in seconds and they flashed away and out of sight.

But that was not the only tiny human-like UFOnauts we have seen reported. In 1970 the international news wires carried a press report of a tiny UFOnaut 3" tall who got out of a three foot UFO and fired a mini-ray at a 10 year old schoolboy, K. Wigneswaran, at a school compound in Penang, Indonesia. That was never followed up with any word and we were left in the dark, to laugh about somebody's prank. However, that was no prank. We can hardly blame everybody who handled that report from cutting it down some to save face. Anybody who would even forward such a report had to be some kind of a nut.

The facts of that matter however, were considerably more profound than ever came through the press filtering process.

Ahmed Jamaludin, a respected UFO investigator in Malaya reported a veritable wave of sighting reports of tiny UFOs, and UFOnauts that got out of little model-sized disc-shaped craft that looked like two big plates placed

THE SECRET UFO CONTACTS OF PAUL VILLA

together at the rims. The flurry of activity that was reported in Malaysia daily in the *Straits Times* and other local papers, was summarized for the 21 and 22 August issues of 1970, and was published in the prestigious British *Flying Saucer Review*, Vol. 28, No. 5, 1983.

Not only was there not just one sighting or one school boy involved, there were many sightings all over Malaya, and many witnesses, and many of the miniature flying discs. The sightings involved schoolboys, teachers, police, military personnel and many others. Up to 25 of the little craft were seen landed in the bushes just outside the school compound at Bukit Mertajan, Penang. From each disc emerged a 3" tall entity. Just as Wigneswaran was closing in for a better look the school bell rang and he had to return to class. That first encounter was in full daylight on the 19th of August 1970.

There were other sightings by six other schoolboys that same evening. One report stated that five little men only 3" tall alighted from a small disc-shaped flying object. One of them was dressed in a yellow suit and the other four wore blue uniforms, they installed an aerial on a tree branch and sent out signals, which frightened the boys and they ran away. More boys went early the next morning to see whether the object was still there, and Mohamed Zulkifli, age 11, reported that the UFO was still there and was surrounded by the little creatures. One eight year old boy reached for one, and was hit by a ray from a tiny weapon, and was struck on the hand, but said it did not hurt much. The boys all went to tell the head teacher of the school, who went back with than but the object was gone.

Wigneswaran went back to the spot at mid-day and found the tiny ship and its occupants again. This time he was shot by the one in the yellow suit when he tried to catch it. He "fainted" after the shooting, and that was where the headmaster later found him, unconsciousness in the bushes. He was carried to the classroom, where he later regained consciousness. A small red dot marked the spot on his right leg where he was shot. The little UFOs and the tiny creatures were seen again by others after class on the 20th. One of the boy's fathers was the police constable for the area. Similar reports came from Rawang in the State of Selangor, from Alor Star in the state of Kedah, Ipoh in the state of Perak, Kampung Pandan in Selangor, Tenroerloh in Pahang, and other locations. One point of interest is that these events were all taking place in the different locations about the same time, and many of them

THE SECRET UFO CONTACTS OF PAUL VILLA

before the first word about them was published. The witnesses in the different places were not in contact with each other. The opportunities for feedback from one story were minimal.

In another case involving mini-UFOs and tiny humanoids was reported from Itaperuna, in the state of Minas Gerais in Brazil. Sr. Benidito Miranda, 48, a chauffeur, who lives with his wife and family of 10 in Cataguases, MG, was on his way home from Itaperuna at 02:00 in the morning of 25 September 1971, a two hour drive, and had come to the heights at the Carangola Bridge on BR 40, when he saw a strange round machine of small size in the middle of the road.

He slowed to pass the unusual vehicle, and as he approached it, he saw two small human-like beings about 30 centimeters (one foot) tall coming out from the interior of the strange craft. These little creatures drew from their belts, a long rolled object looking like a flashlight, and pointed it at him. From this object came a blue light shading to red. When the light struck his body he was suspended weightless in the air. When they increased the intensity of the light he raised more into the air, ascending to some 50 meters. He felt completely paralyzed, nor could he shout for help.

When the lights of another car appeared in the distance, the tiny creatures lowered the beam of light back down to the highway, and Benidito was placed back into his car without using his hands by the power of the light beam caning from the flash-like object. The creatures reentered the small round machine which suddenly took-off with an incredible velocity straight up and was gone. It took Benedito 30 minutes before he was able to move normally and resume driving. He was terribly frightened from being lifted so high with nothing to hang on to.

At 15:00 on 24 September 1972, a truck driver from Las Lunas, New Mexico, was returning from the sanitary fill west of town when he noticed what looked like a flock of strange birds at first. They were flying in an erratic ever-changing formation very low above the desert scrub that grows in that area. Another group of the same things came along right after the first and he now saw that they were small circular bowl-shaped objects with a projecting flange around the base. They were silver in color and quite fast. One of those strange little ships left the formation and approached and passed all around

THE SECRET UFO CONTACTS OF PAUL VILLA

his truck as though inspecting it. While it did so, a bulge began to grow on one side which protruded until it separated itself and became a separate object about the size of a golf ball which flew away. He was able to get pictures of part of this process.

Five years later, in late May 1977, near the same city of Las Lunas, New Mexico, A. Villa, whose wife was away on a visit, was standing at the sink washing dishes when he saw an old truck bed sitting solidly on blocks in the back yard slowly begin to tip up on one side and lay over on its side on the ground. Thinking his young adult son who had gone out to the garden a few minutes before might have done something and be pinned under the truck bed; he rushed out and saw the son in the garden and a small disc-shaped object hovering over the overturned truck. He reached back in the trailer home to get his camera and ran out into the yard and started shooting pictures of the tiny machine.

Mini-UFOs were photographed in the far northern parts of the world also. Jarrro Nykanen was watching the vacant house of his friend while he was away, and in the early afternoon of 16 March, as he was checking on the cottage when he heard a humming sound from behind. Turning, he saw a very small bell-shaped object hovering about two meters above the ground. It looked like the one he had seen at the house six days earlier. It radiated a blue light as it moved forward and ascended and descended alternately. Having his camera with him this time, he started taking photographs and followed it around as he did so. He shot the whole roll of film, 12 pictures, but missed, getting the object in one due to its sometimes jerky movements.

Miniature UFO photographed in 1979 near Suonenjoki, Finland.

THE SECRET UFO CONTACTS OF PAUL VILLA

AALBORG, DENMARK 19 January 1963, 15:15

At about 15:15 in the afternoon of 29 January 1963, Mr. Christian Lynggaard was walking down a street in Aalborg when he noticed what he thought were large soap bubbles floating along beside the parked cars ahead of him...but he became curious when the "soap bubbles" did not break, but persisted in their meandering along the line of parked cars there.

Realizing that this was something different, he opened his camera and began taking pictures. He noticed that the small transparent spheres showed distinct signs of intelligent control and eluded his attempts to capture one. He snapped several pictures of the phenomenon as he watched them before proceeding on his way.

19 January 1963, 15:15, Aalborg, Denmark. Christian Lynggaard snapped several pictures as the small round transparent spheres passed along the line of parked cars as though taking a special interest in them. He thought the objects seemed to be under intelligent control as they did this and then flew away.

THE SECRET UFO CONTACTS OF PAUL VILLA

ALGONDONES, NEW MEXICO 19 June 1966, 09:00

At 09:00 on 19 June 1966, Apolinar Villa was about three miles west of Algondones, and 30 miles north of Albuquerque, when a number of remotely controlled discs and shiny spheres appeared. Some of the discs were about three feet in diameter and some were nearer six feet. The six-foot ones made a loud buzzing noise. The rod sticking up from the top of the dome was not an antenna as might be supposed, but an optical device incorporating a combination of prisms and lenses. It can swivel from the bottom in a circular motion or can simply oscillate from one side to the other, and can be retracted down inside the craft. The movements seem to have something to do with the vivid green light that pulsated inside the disc.

Small mirror shiny spheres about three inches in diameter seemed to rotate around the larger six inch spheres when away from the disc, but when close to it, the larger spheres always remained on top or close to the top. When near the disc the smaller spheres whirled around it in different orbits at different speeds.

The shiny spheres manifest a cascade of changing color from reflective aluminum to gleaming chrome, then to a radiant red or the sparkling blue of an arc welder's torch. With the smaller spheres the color change did not take place rapidly but was gradually modulated from one color to another in a pulsating rhythm. But with the larger spheres the color change was different. As the smaller spheres whirled around the larger ones, the latter changed instantly from shining chrome to luminescent red, blue, green and even yellow. At times the spheres would get glowing hot resembling the infrequently seen and reported "fireballs." Their speed and maneuverability were incredible, for they flitted about like butterflies or raced crazily in high speed orbital patterns.

The witness has seen these spheres in sizes ranging from the tiny three inch ones seen in photos Nos. 4 and 5 up to six to 18 feet in diameter, and he is told that there are giant ones up to an incredible 200 feet in diameter. Some of the discs and sondes have flexible probes resembling the antenna of insects. Larger spheres near power lines have caused electrical failures. Some of the larger four to six foot spheres were captured in photo frames six and seven at about 09:30.

THE SECRET UFO CONTACTS OF PAUL VILLA

19 January 1966, 09:00, Algodones, New Mexico. This silvery disc continued its approach in front of Paul Villa as he snapped photographs of it. The small silvery sphere is making a wide circle above the approaching disc.

19 January 1966, 09:00, Algodones, New Mexico. The relative size of this smaller disc may be judged from its shadow being cast on the ground below it in this picture. Note the shiny sphere orbiting in a circle above the approaching disc.

THE SECRET UFO CONTACTS OF PAUL VILLA

19 January 1966, 09:00, Algondones, New Mexico. As Paul Villa's roll of film was nearly exhausted, on frame 11 for this picture, he waited for the nearest approach of the silvery disc, and then snapped the next to the last picture on his roll of film. Here we can see the disc and its sphere at its closest.

19 January 1966, 09:00, Algondones, New Mexico. At close to 10:00 a 6' sphere circled Paul Villa's car and then took up a position behind it. As Paul was framing the object in the viewfinder the object suddenly exploded with a tremendous boom and seemed to vaporize. Villa caught part of the action on film.

THE SECRET UFO CONTACTS OF PAUL VILLA

At close to 10:00 a larger six foot sphere maneuvered itself around Villa's car as if observing it. The sphere then moved to a position about 150 feet in back of the car. While Villa was framing it in the camera viewfinder for a picture, it suddenly exploded with a tremendous boom and seemed to vaporize. He snapped in a reflex action and got a picture just after the explosion. There was however, no air pressure change of any kind such as would be expected to accompany an explosion.

Towards 11:00 a small three foot disc approached. A small sphere whirled around the top of the disc, sometimes slowly and at other times so fast it seemed to disappear from sight. They both hovered around the witness for a few seconds and then both shot off at great velocity to the east.

At about 12:45 a manned disc about 42 feet in diameter approached and hovered as one individual disembarked and approached. He talked with Villa for about 15 minutes and then went back aboard. The remote discs and spheres flew into the bigger craft and it flew away toward the northeast in a matter of seconds. Villa did not find out if there were any others aboard or not.

One of Villa's photos show a mini-ship, surrounded by silver spheres, extending tripod landing gear in preparation to land.

THE SECRET UFO CONTACTS OF PAUL VILLA

IAS LUNAS, NEW, MEXICO 24 September 1972, 15:00

At about 15:00 in the afternoon of 24 September 1972, Mr. A.V. (declines identification), a truck farmer in Las Lunas, was returning to town from dumping a load of waste at a sand fill scans 15 miles west, when he became involved in a strange event. He was about six miles west of town, driving his pickup vehicle on Highway #6 toward home when, looking to the right, he spotted several small objects "fluttering" along a few dozen feet above the desert scrub there. There were certainly no conventional airplanes because they were too low and too slow. Then he noticed their small size, less than three feet in diameter. They were flying along like a flock of birds with one after another overtaking and then again dropping back as a different one ran ahead.

They were a brightly reflective metallic silver color, circular, and had a wide dome on top of each. As the first group was flying away, a second group of five smaller ones came along behind them. These were about 18 inches in diameter and looked very similar to the others. They all seemed to be intelligently controlled. He stopped his truck and got out with his camera. About the time he was doing that he heard a strange buzz getting louder.

Hurrying, he turned and saw a bigger flying cylinder with three spherical sections to it. It was about 10 feet long by 1.5 feet in diameter, too small to have contained any of these circular craft. It was flying along smoothly with the front end tilted up about 20 to 30 degrees to the line of flight. It also was very low. The spherical sections looked like screen balls around the ends and the middle of the cylinder, and the screens were going through the color changes of heated metal, and the buzz changed with each color change. The cylinder-shaped object was accompanied by four of the smaller disc shapes which were completely silent throughout the whole time.

One of the last discs detached itself from the "flock" and came right toward him at windshield level, stopping instantly in front of his truck. Then it cams right up over the engine hood and hovered as though inspecting the vehicle. He could see that this one was only about 18 inches in diameter. It had a shiny smooth mirror finish and was reflecting the high mid-afternoon sun rays brilliantly. Its raised dome was nearly full width on top surrounded by a narrow rim flange. He could hear no noise from this one.

THE SECRET UFO CONTACTS OF PAUL VILLA

It lowered to fender level as it hovered and slowly rotated around a vertical axis. He noticed a small bulge beginning to grow on one side down near the rim. While he watched this operation the bulge seemed to be getting bigger, the disc moved along the left side of the vehicle and seemed to be inspecting it well, rising and descending as it passed along. It went behind the tailgate and around to the right side, which it also inspected in the same way. The bulge on the side of the object protruded further and then separated into a round mirror bright silver ball about the size of a golf ball which flew around the denied disc several times and then flew away in the direction the others had taken. The silent disc then rose to a higher altitude, hovered a few seconds and then suddenly shot off after the others.

The witness shot the whole roll of film in his camera during this spectacular event, getting seven pictures of the disc and four of the cylinder-shaped object. One photograph of the disc clearly showed the emerging silver ball before it was released and flew away.

A very similar darted disc-shaped object was seen and photographed in that vicinity five years later.

LAS LUNAS, NEW MEXICO – Late May 1977, 09:00

Sometime between 09:00 and 10:00 on a day, late in May 1977, That cannot now be accurately determined, Mr. A. Villa, whose wife was away on a visit, had just finished eating a breakfast snack with his young adult son, and the son had gone out into the garden north of the house to do some work, Villa was standing at the sink, in front of the kitchen window looking out on the back yard to the west. As he was looking out there, he saw a pick-up truck body that was sitting on big blocks against the fence on the south side of the property while he worked on the chassis, begin to slowly roll over to its right (west).

His first reaction was that his son had gone out there and had somehow dislodged one of the blocks and it was rolling over on him – but he could see no sign of his son, and he could see the area of the truck clearly. Then he saw a very small, bright silvery disc wobbling in the air above the truck, which was now lying on its side. As he ran out the door, he grabbed his camera and got

THE SECRET UFO CONTACTS OF PAUL VILLA

24 September 1972, 15:00, Las Lunas, New Mexico. As Paul Villa was returning to town from dumping a load of waste at the landfill, he spotted several small flying objects "fluttering" along a few feet above the desert scrub there. One of the discs detached itself from the "flock" and came right up to the truck.

24 September 1972, 15:00, Las Lunas, New Mexico. One of the 18" diameter discs came right up to the hood of the truck and began hovering around it as Paul Villa, standing out side began shooting pictures of it. This bright silver disc was moved silently as it inspected Villa's truck.

THE SECRET UFO CONTACTS OF PAUL VILLA

24 September 1972, 15:00, Las Lunas, New Mexico. The shiny under surface of the small hi-domed disc was slightly convex and it reflected the red paint of the vehicle in its smooth surface. There were no ports or windows, or protrusions of any kind, and no markings on the external surface of the flying object.

24 September 1972, 15:00, Las Lunas, New Mexico. The domed disc went arount to the rear of Paul Villa's truck. At this point he began to notice a small round raised spot, like a budding blister on the side of the object just above the rim.

THE SECRET UFO CONTACTS OF PAUL VILLA

out just in time to see the shiny circular object still hovering over the truck body off the blocks on its side. The blocks were massive and were very stable with no possibility of this situation accidentally happening. Then he noticed that his son was still in the garden staring at the strange object and its handiwork.

The father began snapping pictures rapidly as the object hovered all about the yard and outbuildings. He managed to get ten pictures in color of the flying object in the air, and one where it momentarily flew inside of the tool shed before it flew away. Then he had his son snap the last pictures of himself and finished the film.

The silver metallic, domed, disc-shaped was about 10 to 12 inches in diameter and had a proportionately wide but smoothly curved dome raised on the upper side. It revolved in a counter-clockwise direction as it moved about, and once launched a still smaller shiny ball that flew around it for a time and then went back inside again. The object seemed to be inspecting them and the yard, and they had the feeling that it was more the observer than the observed.

It flew erratically in the air, and sometimes made very quick changes in direction and speed. They heard no sound caning from it at any time during the observation, it reflected the sun brilliantly, like polished aluminum. They had the feeling that it possessed great power if it wanted to use it.

Examination of the pictures showed no evidence of faking or fraud, no suspensions, no toss-ins or toss-ups, no montages or double exposures, no transparent screens or reflected images, or any of the trick methods available. Shadows and lighting are consistent with the witnesses' story, and internally consistent throughout the picture series. These are real images of structured objects registered properly in the film emulsion layers.

The pictures were made with an economical plastic box camera with a single element fixed focus lens and a standard 1/60th second shutter speed.

The witness insists on protection of his real identity and address as long as he is alive.

Photos obtained from the actual photographer

THE SECRET UFO CONTACTS OF PAUL VILLA

24 September 1972, 15:00, Las Lunas, New Mexico. Paul Villa followed the domed disc as it went around the rear of his vehicle and up along the right side. He could see that the small "blister" was growing as the object proceeded in its inspection. It is seen on the right side of the object here.

24 September 1972, 15:00, Las Lunas, New Mexico. Here the flying object is seen over the rear of Paul Villa's red truck as it continues its inspection of the vehicle. Villa followed it around the vehicle snapping pictures as it proceeded.

THE SECRET UFO CONTACTS OF PAUL VILLA

24 September 1972, 15:00, Las Lunas, New Mexico. The small round "blister" continued to rise on the disc surface just above the rim, until it was a round protrucion, like a big marble, which then detached itself and flew away independently.

24 September 1972, 15:00, Las Lunas, New Mexico. Hearing a strange buzz getting louder, Paul Villa turned and saw a bigger flying cylinder with 3 spherical sections to it. It was about 10 feet long by 1.5 feet in diameter, too small to have contained any of the flying discs.

THE SECRET UFO CONTACTS OF PAUL VILLA

24 September 1972, 15:00, Las Lunas, New Mexico. The spherical sections of the new object looked like screen balls around the ends and middle of the cylindrical object, and the screens were going through color changes, like that of heated metal. The buzz changed with each color change.

24 September 1972, 15:00, Las Lunas, New Mexico. Paul Villa shot a whole roll of film of this event and he got 7 pictures of the disc and 4 of the cylinder-shaped object. One photograph of the disc showed the emerging silver ball before it was released and flew away.

THE SECRET UFO CONTACTS OF PAUL VILLA

Late May 1977. 09:00, Las Lunas, New Mexico. Sometime between 09:00 and 10:00 on a day in late May 1977 Paul Villa was standing at his kitchen window looking out into the back yard when he saw a truckbed roll off its blocks, and he could see a small silvery disc hovering above it.

Late May 1977, 09:00, Las Lunas, New Mexico. Thinking his son who had gone out earlier might be responsible and possibly hurt he called out to him only to find that he was standing in the garden watching the same silvery disc-shaped craft hovering over the tumbled truckbed. Villa grabbed his camera and went out there to see what was going on.

THE SECRET UFO CONTACTS OF PAUL VILLA

Late May 1977, 09:00, Las Lunas, New Mexico. Going out there Paul wondered how the truckbed could have rolled off such solid and stable blocks. The small silvery disc continued to hover about the back yard as Paul and his son inspected the damage. Paul continued to snap pictures of the disc as it hovered.

Late May 1977, 09:00, Las Lunas, New Mexico. Villa continued to snapp pictures as the small silvery disc moved about the yard and outbuildings. The small object momentarily flew inside the tool shed and out again before it flew away. It was about 12 to 18 inches in diameter.

THE SECRET UFO CONTACTS OF PAUL VILLA

Late May 1977, 09:00, Las Lunas, New Mexico. The tiny disc-shaped flying object hovered around some of the other old vehicles in the back yard as though it were inspecting them. It "flitted" rapidly from point to point, like a humming bird. It was of a bright silver color and was completely silent.

Late May 1977, 09:00, Las Lunas, New Mexico. As Paul Villa watched, a small round marble-shaped object of bright silver color emerged from the small disc and flew around it for a time and then went back inside the shiny disc again.

THE SECRET UFO CONTACTS OF PAUL VILLA

Late May 1977, 09:00, Las Lunas, New Mexico. The small shiny disc-shaped object hovered above another old car in the back yard there, apparently taking some kind of special interest in the old vehicles. It was completely silent as it moved about over the cars and buildings out there.

Late May 1977, 09:00, Las Lunas, New Mexico. The tiny silvery disc flew around the outbuildings there in the back yard as though taking an interest in them as well. Paul Villa continued to snap pictures as the mirror-bright disc moved about.

THE SECRET UFO CONTACTS OF PAUL VILLA

Late May 1977, 09:00, Las Lunas, New Mexico. Here the unusual flying object is seen above an abandoned refrigerator that it seemed to inspect along with the old cars and the outbuildings. Paul Villa kept on snapping pictures until the roll of film was almost exhausted.

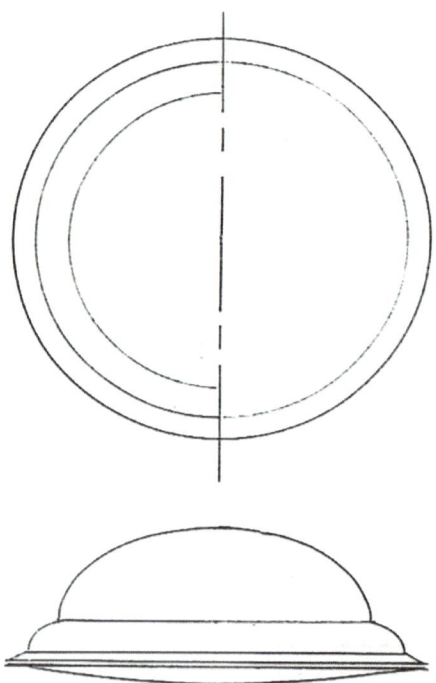

Late May 1977, Las Lunas, New Mexico, 09:00. Line Drawing of the small 18" diameter domed disc that hovered about the back yard of Paul Villas home when a heavy truckbed rolled off its blocks.

THE SECRET UFO CONTACTS OF PAUL VILLA

Paul Villa built his own "UFO" based on the craft he had photographed. It was made from two spun metal discs, that were joined at the rims.

THE SECRET UFO CONTACTS OF PAUL VILLA

CONCLUSION

Our considered judgment of the UFO photographs and the photographer himself and his family lead me to the firm conclusion that Paul Villa captured these pictures just as he described to me. The ones that I have had tested passed all tests as genuine photographs. They have not been altered in any method by any known photographic techniques for faking photographs.

There were no superimpositions, no double exposures, no reflected images, and no paste-ups evident.

Use of models for the smaller craft could not be ruled out, because Paul Villa did actually build a model with two spun metal discs joined at the rims, and with broomstick legs, suggested by his visitors. They had him take it to a deserted location for a demonstration.

Suddenly the sky filled with shiny mirror-finish metallic-looking balls flying all around. One…about four inches in diameter came down and orbited in a small circle above the model and it rose into the air.

Paul grabbed his camera and photographed that flying object while the shiny sphere hovered above it. The shadow cast on the ground under that model object clearly shows its diameter as about 24 inches and above the tire track in the photo. The small sphere carried it all around that place and then brought it back.

That was the only model I ever saw there in his possession.

His initial reply to Coral Lorenzen's barbed question was of course false at the time and was a retaliatory remark, because from that he knew that they did not come for facts as much as they wanted to expose him as a fraud.

Paul had a lot of Indian blood in him and he believed in fair treatment of everyone until they demonstrated unfairness in themselves. When they did that, he gave them like in return, and never fully trusted them again.

THE SECRET UFO CONTACTS OF PAUL VILLA

Circa November, 1968...many believe Paul Villa took this photo. It was actually snapped over Grants Pass, Oregon and is generally credited to Tahalita Fry, who was married to Daniel Fry. The well known contactees may have actually taken the picture, but for personal reasons decided to give credit to his spouse.

PAUL VILLA – THE MODEST CONTACTEE

By Tim R. Swartz

The contactee movement that started in the early 1950s was partly due to the growing media attention to the worldwide explosion of UFO sightings. In the beginning, it was feared that UFOs were some sort of advanced aircraft from a foreign power (the Soviet Union if you were American, the U.S. if you were Russian). However, this theory was pretty quickly dashed as reports poured in describing the objects incredible speed and maneuverability...which were far beyond anything, cutting edge science or not, that humans had accomplished at that point.

It wasn't long though before the idea started to spread that UFOs could be spaceships from some other planet; and very quickly, people came forward claiming that they were the recipients of interplanetary visitations. UFO researchers, who wanted more than anything for the subject to be taken seriously, loathed the contactees and the ideas that they represented.

Most of the major players in the contactee movement were a cross between new age shamans and carnival barkers. The Space Brothers were here to help us make that next leap in evolution, away from war, hate and atomic weapons...to peace and love, in preparation to joining up with other, friendly planets throughout the cosmos.

A few of the early contactees, like George Adamski, made money from their books and speaking engagements. However, if anyone became a "contactee" thinking it was their path to riches and glory, they were sadly mistaken. Adam Gorightly and Greg Bishop have written an excellent book on this subject, "***A is For Adamski***," and I highly recommend it.

THE SECRET UFO CONTACTS OF PAUL VILLA

Apolinar (Paul) Villa was somewhat of a late-comer to the whole contactee thing. Even though he claimed that his first meeting with the "spacemen" happened in 1953, it wasn't until the mid-1960s that his story, along with his photographed became public.

From all accounts is seems that Villa was very much a reluctant contactee. His encounters are almost textbook examples of the "typical contactee meeting." In his interviews, Villa talks of friendly space people who are beautiful, almost angelic, in appearance, offering up explanations on how the universe works and what role planet Earth plays within it. But Villa didn't hit the UFO conference circuit to promote his experiences, or sell photos. He pretty much stayed quiet about the whole affair unless he was asked first.

Thanks to Gabriel Green and his *"International UFO Journal,"* Villa's photographs became widely publicized, yet at that time, almost nothing was known about the man who took them. Col. Wendelle Stevens, the author of this book, actually took the time to visit Villa at his home and listen to his story without passing immediate judgment.

For the most part, Paul Villa shunned publicity, refusing to talk with the press, or with UFO researchers. He claimed that his life had been threatened and once someone even took a shot at him while he was in his pickup truck. Those who did talk with him found him credible. The late Bill Sherwood, who was an optical physicist and a senior project development engineer for the Eastman-Kodak company, said that "Villa never tried to use his unusual personal experiences for monetary gain. To me he seemed always humble and sincere; unimpressed by the attention he received from the Secretary-General of the United Nations, U Thant, who called him at his workshop to discuss his experiences with the extraterrestrials."

Researcher and author Timothy Good also spent time with Villa in 1976 and was told that there were three different groups of extraterrestrial beings visiting Earth, including "certainly one that is good." Villa stated that the space people had hundreds of bases within our solar system, including many of Earth, Mars and the moon. Some groups came here simply as tourists. Villa's group worked with about 70 contactees in the U.S. and about 300 worldwide. Unfortunately, there is still a lot of information about Villa's contacts that will never be known.

THE SECRET UFO CONTACTS OF PAUL VILLA

In his book, "**Alien Bases**," Timothy Good wrote about when Villa drove him and Lou Zinsstag to one of the sites beside the Rio Grande near Algodones. It was this location where he had taken photos of the craft and spoke with its occupants (who would not allow themselves to be photographed).

Good asked what the other members of the crew were doing while Villa spoke with the man he assumed was the pilot.

"Oh they were just bathing their feet in the river," Villa replied.

Good wrote that this matter-of-fact statement helped convince him that Paul Villa's story contained essential elements of truth. As with other contactees' stories, there seems to be a mix of truth and fiction and it can be almost impossible to find where one ends and the other begins.

Paul Villa passed away in 1981. Before he died, Villa had shown Wendelle Stevens a footlocker full of notes and unpublished photographs, promising that after he passed away, Stevens could have them. In one folder, there were allegedly photographs that Villa had shot on another planet (something that was never revealed in any detail while he was alive). Villa said that he had been taken to this planet by his space friends and had shot a series of photos that showed two dinosaur-like beasts, tan and brown splotched in color, with long necks and tails, grazing on the tops of moderate sized trees.

Stevens said the photos were so good that he could see the rippling muscles and wrinkles in the neck skin of the animal where it turned its head. The whole scene, including the other vegetation and sparse grass on a near desert ground was most realistic, and was certainly not a painting. There were three or four of these photographs in close sequence in that series.

Sadly, after Villa's death, his wife Eunis sold their trailer and furnishings and moved away. Stevens was unable to track her down and the fate of Villa's lost photos and notes is unknown.

Like many other UFO contact cases, we are left to ponder the strange circumstances of the reluctant contactee Paul Villa and his mysterious friends from beyond.

THE SECRET UFO CONTACTS OF PAUL VILLA

The magic of Paul Villa's Space Brother friends dates back into antiquity.
Inspired art © by Carol Ann Rodriguez.

ITALY'S "FRIENDSHIP" CASE

By Sean Casteel - From the Book *"UFO Repeaters"*

Unknown to Paul Villa (and practically everyone else in the world) there was a mass contact event taking shape in and around the Italian town of Pescara. It was the 1950s, when flying saucers seemed to be everywhere in the skies over Italy, sometimes being photographed, sometimes inducing fear and a mild public hysteria. For a long time, the phenomenon of "contactism," or the deliberate encounter, repeated over time, between man and extraterrestrials was believed to involve only a few chosen individuals or "contactees."

But in 2007, that picture would be altered when researcher and author Stefano Breccia published some startling papers that revealed the story of repeated direct encounters between more than 100 people and extraterrestrial beings living in numerous secret bases on our planet.

JOURNALIST PAOLA HARRIS TELLS THE STORY

In the summer of 2013, my sometimes writing partner, John Weigle, and I covered a lecture delivered by Italian-American journalist Paola Harris to the Close Encounter Research Organization in Thousand Oaks, California. (Paola had also been on the scene of and affirmed a sighting by Antonio Urzi.) In her lecture, Paola covered the story of the "Friendship" case in some detail.

The story begins with the aforementioned Stefano Breccia, who first brought the case to light after several of the participants came forward to discuss their experiences with him.

Eyewitnesses to the Friendship case (which took place from around 1956 to 1990) told Breccia about human-looking aliens who spoke perfect Italian, among many other languages. Much like the beautiful extraterrestrials that visited with Paul Villa, the Friendship beings explained

THE SECRET UFO CONTACTS OF PAUL VILLA

This photo is allegedly an over 8 foot tall "Friendship" extraterrestrial and was taken in 1976 by Professor Bruno Sammaciccia, a Catholic historian with degrees in psychology and psychiatry.

that the Earth had been created for a positive purpose but that man was turning everything into evil. The level of human morality was much lower than their own, they said, and they were there to ensure the situation didn't get out of hand. They had not come to conquer, as there was nothing to conquer, but instead emphasized that all things required love and respect and that everything should be done in accordance with these principles. The aliens also said they were familiar with Earth's history and its differing religions.

Breccia was told the aliens had already been here for many years and had lived at secret bases in various places on the planet. They preferred not to reveal themselves publicly because people weren't ready for contact. Breccia himself met with many of the aliens. Some of them were very tall, including one alien who was 15-feet-tall and was photographed towering over some trees in the background.

The aliens were given the name "W-56s" because the year they initially made contact with the Pescara group was 1956. The W-56s are a confederation of different people coming from throughout nearly all of the known universe. To them, the Earth has a mystical meaning because it is among the only fifty Mother Planets where life has been born. But we are not evolved enough, Harris reiterated, to meet this cosmic consciousness in a spirit of complete understanding.

One woman who took part in the contact said, "We were hoping for an experience with teachers who could help us love."

THE SECRET UFO CONTACTS OF PAUL VILLA

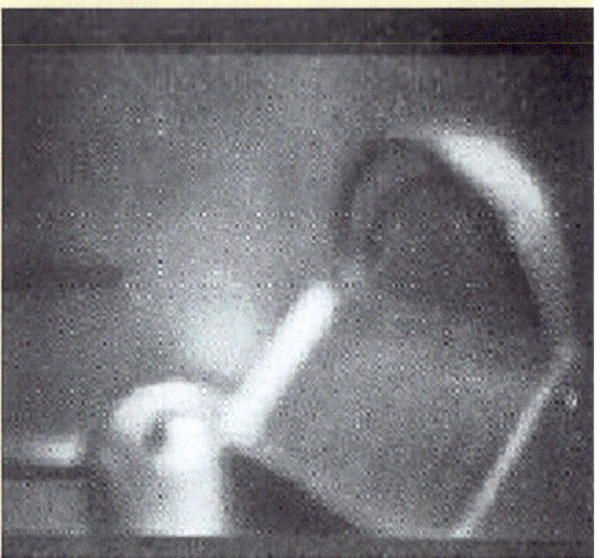

In October 1957, a UFO landed near Francavilla, Italy. Two men were allowed to enter the disc and take photographs of not only the interior of the ship, but also of its extraterrestrial pilot. The photos were originally published in the book "*Sono Extraterrestrial*" (They are Extraterrestrials!) in 1958 by Dr. Alberto Perego.

The photos are also included in the 2018 book "*UFO Contacts In Italy*," published by Flying Disc Press.

THE SECRET UFO CONTACTS OF PAUL VILLA

Meetings between the humans and the ETs continued for several months. At one point, the "Friends" started asking for help and wanted industrial quantities of fruits and vegetables of various kinds. After taking delivery of a truckload of produce, the truck driver was lured away by the invitation to share coffee with the humans, at which point the aliens teleported the goods off the truck. The driver was surprised to return and find the truck was already empty.

A BELIEVER WITH NOTHING TO PROVE

Breccia would come to write a book about the Friendship case called "***Mass Contacts: The 1950s Contact In Pescara, Italy, With Human-Looking Aliens***." When Paola interviewed Breccia for her own book, "***Exopolitics: All The Above***," he told her that "I do not intend that anybody believes what I have written. It's up to the reader to decide whether I am a fool or not. About the photos, I am the first one to state that the pictures are meaningless. I even present a fake, done by myself. I've included a lot of pictures simply because most of them are totally unknown, up to now. Think of the scout craft formation, seen from above! Or the many pictures shot during a landing. I've never seen anything like that in any UFO book, therefore I believe **'Contattismi di Massa'** has been the first one to show such things. There are even two pictures of W-56 people."

According to Breccia, there are bases near Pescara on the Adriatic Coast which he finds difficult to describe because of technology we don't understand. He says, however, there are no fixed entries to them; when necessary, a passageway is opened, and then closed, and everything goes back to the "status quo." The largest base had a ceiling 300 meters high, and sometimes it rained inside the base.

"A lot of [the aliens] are living among us, interacting at ease with our society, having Earth identities," Breccia said, adding that the beings he had interacted with had left "a very friendly" impression.

Which, much to our relief, seems to be the general pattern among UFO Repeaters such as Paul Villa. The aliens who return to certain contactees again and again do indeed seem to be trying to establish some kind of "friendship" with that individual, to slowly create an atmosphere of comfort

THE SECRET UFO CONTACTS OF PAUL VILLA

and trust. They even seem to want some of the contactees to meet them with a camera in their hands and are willing to "pose" for a few photos.

Perhaps it's all about creating a "family album" to enable future generations to look back at the early days when contact was still in its infancy?

Those fascinated by the Paul Villa case should watch the documentary *"The Friendship Case: The Extraordinary Experience of Contact with Aliens in Italy,"* available on Amazon Prime and other streaming services.

This documentary explores the extraordinary story of mass alien contact that has been kept secret for half a century. For almost 20 years, a group of extraterrestrials contacted hundreds of people with a number of strange requests. The project was called "Friendship."

The first Friendship case meeting between eight and three foot tall extraterrestrials with three Italian witnesses.

THE SECRET UFO CONTACTS OF PAUL VILLA

The people involved were taken on board multiple UFOs and also shown alien bases on earth. These people are of high social and cultural importance...among them, the Italian diplomat Alberto Perego.

The witnesses of this incredible alien contact are finally willing to speak. This documentary changes past assumptions of why interaction between humans and extraterrestrial civilizations exist. Includes stunning photos and film footage of alien spacecraft in flight.

The contacts took place in Pescara, and writer Bruno Samaciccia was considered the main contactee. Two other people involved, Gaspare De Lama and his wife Mirella, are alive today. Breccia's respected status in academia and science inspired Gaspare to come forward with his story.

Bruno referred to the off-world humans with whom he made contact as the W56. The "W" stood for "double victory" and was also a reference to George Washington. The W56 were a group of humans who came from various parts of the cosmos. Beyond being scientifically and spiritually advanced and taller than people on our planet (they ranged from one to six meters in height), they were a lot like us.

http://in5d.com/the-friendship-case-evidence-of-extraterrestrial-contact

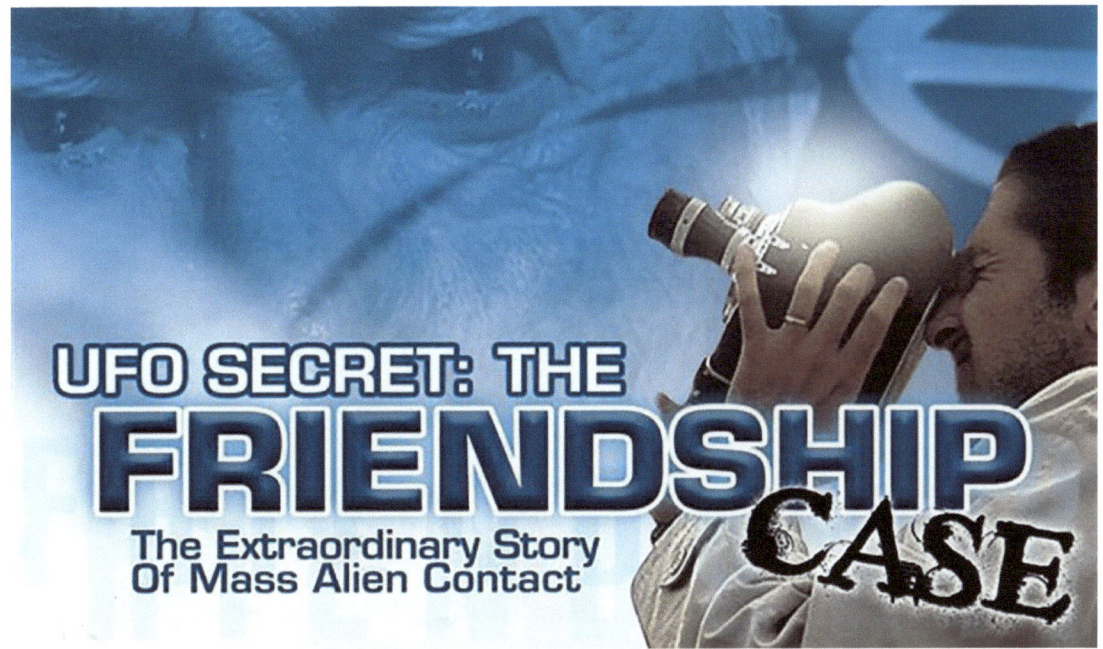

Poster for the documentary "*The Friendship Case: The Extraordinary Experience of Contact with Aliens in Italy.*"

THE SECRET UFO CONTACTS OF PAUL VILLA

ABOUT THE AUTHOR

Lt. Colonel Wendelle C. Stevens was a leading ufologist for more than 50 years and the creator of one of the largest private UFO photo archives known. Stevens' interest in the UFO phenomenon was kindled by his experience as an Air Force pilot in the Arctic after the end of World War II, where he encountered mysterious radio transmissions while working as part of a classified project to photograph and map the area using new technology.

Stevens began his own investigations after retiring from the Air Force and in 1979 published the 4-volume "***UFO Contact from the Pleia***des," which detailed the extraterrestrial experiences of Edouard "Billy" Meier in Germany and established Stevens' reputation in the world of Ufology.

Over the following three decades, Stevens amassed his collection of UFO photographs from around the world, researching and writing articles about the encounter stories they illustrated and appearing as an expert at UFO conferences internationally.

From his home in Tucson, he was the Director of Investigations for the Aerial Phenomena Research Organization (APRO) and a founder of the International UFO Congress. In total, Stevens authored or co-authored more than 22 UFO-related monographs. Colonel Stevens received a lifetime achievement award at the First World UFO Forum in Brasilia, 1997. He passed away in Tucson, Arizona, in 2010.

THE SECRET UFO CONTACTS OF PAUL VILLA

LARGEST INDEPENDENT PUBLISHER OF ALTERNATIVE BOOKS SINCE 1965

EXPLORE THESE "WAY-OUT" WORLDS

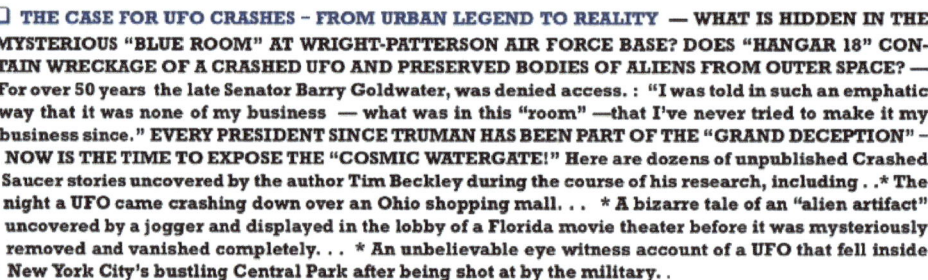

NEW RELEASE!

❑ **PROJECT MAGNET — THE LIGHTS IN THE SKY ARE NOT STARS!**
ONE MAN ALONE IS SAID TO HOLD THE KEY TO THE SECRETS OF THE FLYING SAUCERS AND HOW THEY ARE ABLE TO PERFORM INCREDIBLE MANEUVERS IN OUR ATMOSPHERE — AND HE CLAIMS THEY HAVE ESTABLISHED FACE-TO-FACE CONTACT WITH HUMANS. HERE IS THE COMPLETE TOP-SECRET HISTORY OF UFOS AND HUMANOID SIGHTINGS IN CANADA.

Wilbert B. Smith was a Canadian engineer responsible for the technical aspects of broadcasting between the U.S and his country during the 1950s. Because of the number of UFO sightings over Canadian air space, Smith convinced his government to establish a UFO monitoring system, which eventually did detect anomalous phenomena in the sky which Smith felt certain was of an off-world origin. Dying of cancer, Smith made arrangements with his wife to hide his "sensitive" files so they would not fall into the hands of those who would use his findings for their own unscrupulous ends. "They will be coming to ransack all my work," Smith proclaimed. And he was right! As predicted, Canadians, Americans and Soviets approached his widow, requesting she turn over her husband's work as it would help to further expedite their unprincipled labors. Tales of crashed saucers. Human looking ETs here now. Govt sponsored cover ups. ❑ **$19.95**

❑ **THE CASE FOR UFO CRASHES – FROM URBAN LEGEND TO REALITY** — WHAT IS HIDDEN IN THE MYSTERIOUS "BLUE ROOM" AT WRIGHT-PATTERSON AIR FORCE BASE? DOES "HANGAR 18" CONTAIN WRECKAGE OF A CRASHED UFO AND PRESERVED BODIES OF ALIENS FROM OUTER SPACE? — For over 50 years the late Senator Barry Goldwater, was denied access. : "I was told in such an emphatic way that it was none of my business — what was in this "room" —that I've never tried to make it my business since." EVERY PRESIDENT SINCE TRUMAN HAS BEEN PART OF THE "GRAND DECEPTION" – NOW IS THE TIME TO EXPOSE THE "COSMIC WATERGATE!" Here are dozens of unpublished Crashed Saucer stories uncovered by the author Tim Beckley during the course of his research, including . .* The night a UFO came crashing down over an Ohio shopping mall. . . * A bizarre tale of an "alien artifact" uncovered by a jogger and displayed in the lobby of a Florida movie theater before it was mysteriously removed and vanished completely. . . * An unbelievable eye witness account of a UFO that fell inside New York City's bustling Central Park after being shot at by the military. .

❑ **Order CASE FOR UFO CRASHES, $22.00. Includes bonus DVD.**

❑ **THE ASTOUNDING UFO SECRETS OF JIM MOSELEY** INCLUDES FULL TEXT OF UFO CRASH SECRETS AT WRIGHT PATTERSON AIR FORCE BASE — THIS IS NOT JUST ANOTHER BOOK ABOUT UFO SIGHTINGS OR THE CRASH AT ROSWELL! — IT'S AN EXTRAORDINARY REMEMBRANCE OF THE COURT JESTER — THE GRAND TROUBADOUR — THE NUMERO UNO TRICKSTER — OF ALL OF UFOLOGY. In addition to the musings and gossip of those that he remained closest to in life, Jim (with the help of endeared drinking buddy and ghost writer Gray Barker) fans out across the country to personally investigate some of the most perplexing UFO cases of all time –Cases personally pondered over by Moseley in this book include: ** "I Met Two Men From 'Venus' — And They Had No Fingerprints!" ** What Happened To The "Authentic" UFO Film That Vanished Without A Trace? ** Kidnapped By Aliens? – A Most Strange And Unusual Case. ** The Angels Of Oahspe. ** Adamski, Williamson And The Case For The UFO Contactees. ** Behind The Barbed Wire Fence At Wright-Patterson Air Force Base. ** The OSI And The Lubbock Lights. ** ETs And Alien Wreckage - The Strange Story Of An Air Force Whistleblower. ** The Earth Theory And UFOs From The Antarctica.

❑ **Order SECRETS OF JIM MOSELEY -$20.00**

❑ **UMMO AND THE EXTRATERRESTRIAL PAPERS** — THE ALIENS ARE AMONG US! THEY WISH TO COMMUNICATE! AND HAVE EVEN CONSTRUCTED CITIES IN REMOTE PLACES WHILE THEY ARE HERE! The story of UMMO starts with a series of letters and phone calls to various Spanish UFO researchers in 1965 that purportedly came from an extraterrestrial race. While the most commonly reported method of ET contact is clearly by telepathy, the aliens in this case tried a more direct, decidedly earthly method of communication. The letters contained highly detailed discourses on such weighty topics as physics and medicine that could only have been written by experts on the cutting edge in those rarified fields that are light years beyond what a lay hoaxer could have come up with. One of the letters also predicted that a UFO sighting would occur on a certain day at a certain location in Spain, and the ship did indeed appear on schedule and at the appointed place. Photos of their ships and unique symbol have been taken as added verification. A similar account has popped up in Canada and is included. This book is over 250 large size pages and contains never before revealed info on this fascinating episode. ❑ **Order UMMO AND THE ET PAPERS - $25.00**

❑ **SUPER SPECIAL –ORDER ALL ITEMS THIS PAGE - $69.00 + $8 S/H AND WE WILL INCLUDE A BONUS DVD ON AN INTRIGUING ASPECT OF THE UFO MYSTERY**

Timothy Beckley, Box 753, New Brunswick, NJ 08903

THE SECRET UFO CONTACTS OF PAUL VILLA

Unsolved Mysteries! Hidden History! Unexplained Phenomena! Censored Events!

☐ **UFO REPEATERS—THE CAMERA DOESN'T LIE!— $24.00**
Here are the fantastic but true accounts of people from Turkey to New York City who claim repeated contact with Ultra-terrestrials. What makes their experiences so unique are the photos as evidence of their claims. Not blurry shots, but real hardware that came, they say, from space. Many have had numerous encounters, including Howard Menger, Marc Brinkerhoff, Ellen Crystal and Paul Villa.

☐ **SPOOKY TREASURE TROVES: UFOS, GHOSTS, CURSED PIECES OF EIGHT AND THE SUPERNATURAL — $20.00**
From the Oak Island Knights Templar connection to the billion dollar Cocoas Island loot, paranormal manifestations have beckoned many to hidden treasures. Or these same spirits can lead you to an early grave to keep their secrets. Native American legends from AZ. Super Psychic Ted Owens in NM. Superstition Mountains. Kick ass book.
Over 300 large format pages.

☐ **T.LOBSANG RAMPA TRILOGY Famed Tibetan "Walk-In." 3 Best Sellers! - $29.00**
"The Hermit" — Secrets passed down by mysterious "Higher Order" who have protected and guided Earth since creation. *"Tibetan Sage"* — The Lama probes the history of our planet as he reenters the cave of the ancients and taken on a tour of the Hall of Records. *"Three Lives"* — Rampa delves deep into the magical realm of the human soul and immortality. Bonus Prayer-Meditation CD.

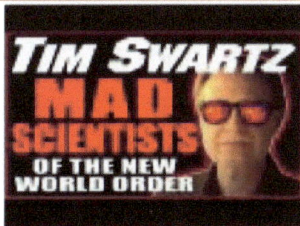
☐ **THE FINAL NAIL IN YOUR COFFIN! — $15.00**
A pox to all of mankind. Morgellons and Red Mercury Plagues may have been created in NWO Labs of "Mad Scientists." Emmy Award winning producer Tim Swartz delves into two modern conspiracies. Russians? Area 51?: Secret Order?

☐ **UFOS, TIME SLIPS, OTHER REALMS, THE SCIENCE OF FAIRIES — $15.00**
Here is your personal passport to the wonderland of Magonia. Another world awaits just beyond the realm of consciousness. A different explanation for the Saucer People. "Little Men" are NOT from Mars! "Banned" by "serious" researchers!
☐ Elfan Fairy Spell Pendant—**Add $20**

☐ **BIBLICAL UFO REVELATIONS and SEARCH FOR THE PALE PROPHET — $25.00**
Rev. Barry Downing says ET powers caused ancient miracles and both Testaments are manifestations of an alien intelligence. Was Jesus\sent from another planet? Sean Casteel asks: Who was the mysterious robe-clad healer who walked about the tribes of America 2000 years ago? —2 books.

☐ **ANCIENT ASTRONAUTS 3 BOOK SET — $29.95**
By George Hunt Williamson. *"The Saucers Speak."* Calling all occupants of interplanetary craft. No need to set up huge telescopes or communicate via SETI. They can speak to you now! *"Other Tongues, Other Flesh."* The Wanderers, the Migrants, The Prophets, the Harvesters. The Agents are here! *"Traveling The Path Back To The Road In The Sky."* Strange saga of saucers, space brothers and secret agents.

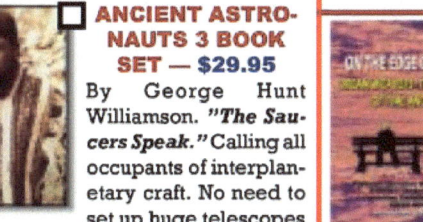
☐ **ON THE EDGE OF REALITY: DREAM WEAVERS — MASTERS OF TIME AND SPACE — $15.00**
Brent Raynes says there are Ant People, Snake People, Blue People, Star People, Tricksters and "flying ghosts!" Probe secret sites, and earthworks where strange energies and balls of intelligent light manifest. Learn how to wire the brain to process a paranormal-interdimensional experience.

☐ **OUT OF THE DARKNESS — $15.00**
Our planet is in great jeopardy! Psychics and Prophets offer shocking news about our future. Are we about to enter a new dimension of consciousness — or are we about to be blindsided by a series of unexplained, tragic, events? Is Planet X coming our way? Storms? Massive power failures? Can we avoid such frightening events?

☐ **SPECIAL — ALL ITEMS THIS AD JUST $148.00 + $15.00 S/H**
TIMOTHY BECKLEY, BOX 753, NEW BRUNSWICK, NJ 08903
24/7 Credit Cards 646 331-6777 (Private cell phone. Orders only. Leave all information (and your number).
mrufo8@hotmail.com for PayPal Invoices

www.ingramcontent.com/pod-product-compliance
Lightning Source LLC
Chambersburg PA
CBHW042023150426
43198CB00002B/49